COMPOSITIONAL TRANSITIONS IN 1 PETER

AN ANALYSIS OF THE LETTER-OPENING

PHILIP L. TITE

COMPOSITIONAL TRANSITIONS IN 1 PETER

AN ANALYSIS OF THE LETTER-OPENING

PHILIP L. TITE

International Scholars Publications
San Francisco - London - Bethesda
1997

Library of Congress Cataloging-in-Publication Data

Tite Philip L., 1969-
    Compositional transitions in 1 Peter : an analysis of the letter
    -opening / Philip Tite.
        p. cm.
    Includes bibliographical references and index.
    ISBN 1-57309-148-0 (alk. paper) -- ISBN 1-57309-147-2 (pbk. :
    alk. paper)
    1. Bible. N.T. Peter, 1st I, 1-14—Language, style. I. Title.
    II. Title: Compositional transitions in First Peter.
    BS2795.2.T58   1997
    227'.9206—DC21   96-52503
                                                         CIP

Editorial Inquiries:
International Scholars Publications
7831 Woodmont Avenue, #345
Bethesda, MD 20814

To order: (800) 55-PUBLISH

In Loving Memory of My Grandparents

The Rev. Harold and Pattie Tite

who first introduced me to the sacrificial love of Christ

FOREWORD

This study tells us much about its author, whom I have known now for almost a decade, having had the pleasure of watching him develop into an outstanding young academic. It is Philip Tite's first book and one need not be a prophet to know that it will not be his last.

Tite shows a marked fascination here with transitions. He explores the way the author of 1 Peter has skilfully created a text whose sections lead effectively into one another, the linking words moving the argument forward incrementally, giving new meaning to the surrounding passages. The spotlight is directed to these transitional elements in the letter's opening section, but in the process what is revealed in 1:1-14 about 1 Peter's rhetorical art applies to the letter as a whole. Tite himself has embodied this reality over the years - - linking church and academic interests, the non-canonical sources with the canonical and the "heretical" with the "orthodox" - - to arrive at a view of Christian origins that is as fluid and transformative as 1 Peter's.

Readers will also notice the author's deep interest in academic discourse. As the footnotes alone reveal, Tite has studied all the secondary literature he can on 1 Peter, and he expects as much from others. To read this book is to engage the field of Petrine studies. Building primarily on the work of his teacher, Troy Martin, Tite's analysis reflects the discipline required to appreciate another person's theory and the courage needed to modify it when deemed necessary. This stance is quintessential "Tite," as his oral presentations and other publications to date have shown.

The same can be said for his attention to the biblical texts, which for him are always primary. Although no reading can ever strictly be "objective," this is not a book about what he himself would like to see in this under-explored New

i

Testament letter, nor does it simply reflect his teacher's views; rather, it is a study of what he can find in the text itself, set in its religio-historical context. Consequently, the reader will emerge from this book with more than a sound knowledge of those opening verses in 1 Peter, which by themselves are intriguing only to a handful of scholars. His broad approach to the texts is what will linger. Tite's exegetical gifts, to paraphrase 1 Peter 4:10, indeed serve us well.

Michel Desjardins
Associate Professor
Department of Religion and Culture
Wilfrid Laurier University

ACKNOWLEDGMENTS

No endeavour is accomplished on one's own merits. I owe a great debt of gratitude to various individuals for their role in bringing this book to completion. This project began in 1993 as a Masters thesis at Olivet Nazarene University. Since then, it has grown into its current state of existence. I would like to express my appreciation to my advisor, Larry Murphy, for his continual guidance throughout this project. Other individuals within the Division of Religion at Olivet also deserve a word of gratitude. I think specifically of Richard Thompson, Robert Branson, and Russell Lovett. During my explorations of 1 Peter, provocative and insightful discussions occurred during two paper presentations of my material: "Rhetorical Criticism in 1 Peter" at the University of Toronto Colloquim on Religions of Classsical Antiquity, January 19, 1996; and "The Compositional Debate in 1 Peter Studies" at the AAR/Eastern International Region, LeMoyne College, Syracuse, April 13, 1996. I appreciate all those who took part in those sessions. I also extend my thanks to Troy Martin for our many talks on 1 Peter. His inspiration is perhaps his greatest contribution to this project. I also appreciated my talks with Peter Davids, both in Chicago and over the phone. I greatly appreciated his assistance in my obtaining certain research material. Also, thanks are due Robert Webb and Peter Erb for their assistance. My brief conversation with Paul Achtemeier this past April was also very enlightening. It is unfortunate that his recent commentary on 1 Peter was not accessible during the writing of this book. Michel Desjardins, who kindly agreed to write a Foreword for this work, has been a wonderful friend, offering encouragement and guidance to me not only during my work on 1 Peter but throughout my academic career. Others who were moral support throughout this project were Peter Richardson, Ken Derry, Jeffrey Enfield, Tony S. L. Michael,

Arlene MacDonald, Andrea Frolic, Lorraine VanderHoef, Sonya Janzen, Eric Van Dusen, Daniel McFeeley, Jeremy Thompson, Gordon Armstrong, Kip Slayback, Eric Smith, Efton Elliott, Dan Farr, and, not to be forgotten, my dear sister Kim and my new borther-in-law Larry. I wish also to say "thank you" to the staff and workers of Benner Library, most notable Kathy Van Fossan and the Interlibrary Loan Department. In reference to the latter, Belinda McConnell deserves special mention. I further appreciate the staff of the Fischer Rare Book Library in Toronto for granting me access to their collection. Without the gracious assistance of these libraries, this book would not have been possible. The ONU Computer Center, especially Dennis Seymour, was very helpful throughout the various drafts of this work. A note of appreciation is well earned by the staff at International Scholars Publications, most notably Robert West, for their kindness in bringing this book to published form. I wish to thank my parents, Larry and Gayle Tite, for their love and financial support throughout my academic career. The love and kindness of the Limestone Church of the Nazarene and the Cambridge Preston Church of the Nazarene has been an invaluable asset in bringing this project to completion. I wish to express a special word of appreciation to Raquel Menendez for her constant friendship and prayers over the last few years. As I write this acknowledgement, I am reminded that this book is not the product of one person, and that the joys of life are best shared. *Merci* to one and all!

Philip L. Tite
Department of Religion and Culture
Wilfrid Laurier University
Waterloo, Ontario
June 1996

ABBREVIATIONS

AB	Anchor Bible
AJBI	*Annual of the Japanese Biblical Institute*
AJP	*American Journal of Philology*
ANRW	*Aufstieg und Niedergang der römischen Welt*
ATR	*Anglican Theological Review*
AusBR	*Australian Biblical Review*
BAR	*Biblical Archaeology Review*
Bib	*Biblica*
BSac	*Bibliotheca Sacra*
BTB	*Biblical Theology Bulletin*
CBC	Cambridge Bible Commentary
CBQ	*Catholic Biblical Quarterly*
CJ	*The Classical Journal*
ConcorJ	*Concordia Journal*
ConNT	*Coniectanea neotestamentica*
CW	*Classical World*
EvQ	*Evangelical Quarterly*
ExpTim	*Expository Times*
FilologiaNT	*Filologia Neotestamentaria*
GJ	*Grace Journal*
Greg	*Gregorianum*
HTR	*Harvard Theological Review*
IB	Interpreter's Bible
Int	*Interpretation*
JBL	*Journal of Biblical Literature*
JETS	*Journal of the Evangelical Theological Society*
JSNT	*Journal for the Study of the New Testament*
JSNTSup	Journal for the Study of the New Testament -- Supplement Series
JTS	*Journal of Theological Studies*
LCL	Loeb Classical Library
LD	Lectio divina
NABPR	National Associatiion of Baptist Professors of Religion
Neot	*Neotestamentica*
NIBC	New International Bible Commentary
NovT	*Novum Testamentum*
NTS	*New Testament Studies*
PrincSB	*The Princeton Seminary Bulletin*

TABLE OF CONTENTS

CHAPTER ONE:

METHODOLOGICAL CONSIDERATIONS

INTRODUCTION

Of all the writings produced by the early Christians, 1 Peter is one of the most aesthetically powerful. The ingenious interplay of imagery, quotations, and allusions makes this relatively short New Testament letter a magnificent example of early Christian artistry. Sometimes considered underdeveloped in its theological sophistication, 1 Peter is deceptively sophisticated.[1] Indeed, the imaginative process within this text reveals both the creativity of the author as well as the imaginative reaction it must have evoked. The reaction of wonder that this little letter must have evoked among early Christians has also been felt by others throughout the centuries. Martin Luther, as one example, referred to 1 Peter as "one of the noblest books in the New Testament: it is the genuine and pure Gospel."[2]

Since John H. Elliott first called 1 Peter an "exegetical step-child"[3] in 1976, scholarly attention on 1 Peter has increased significantly. Indeed, the tide

---

[1]As an example of this negative view of 1 Peter in academia, David Dungan ("The Purpose and Provenance of the Gospel of Mark According to the 'Two-Gospel' (Griesbach) Hypothesis," *Colloquy on New Testament Studies: A Time for Reappraisal and Fresh Approaches*, ed. by Bruce Corley [Macon, GA: Mercer University Press, 1983 (including a "Seminar Dialogue with David Dungan")], 158), in the discussion of his paper correlating 1 Peter and Mark, described his own experience in the classroom as follows: "So I have to confess to everyone, this was the first time I carefully examined 1 Peter and the recent research associated with it. I had just sort of skipped over it in graduate school because our teachers put it down as essentially a document of clichés. They told us that the beautiful phrases never lead anywhere, that 1 Peter in no way resembled the intellectual depth of the genuine letters of Paul. As my teacher, Krister Stendahl, said one time, 'Deep down 1 Peter is shallow.' So, with this block in mind, I never read 1 Peter or studied it or anything." Dungan's experience (which was reversed with the production of his Mark-1 Peter paper) typifies both the attitude within the field of scholarship as well as the classroom, where the next generation of scholarship is being molded. Petrine scholars have worked hard, with mixed success, to raise the status of 1 Peter in Christian origins.

[2]Martin Luther, "Sermons on the First Epistle of St. Peter," trans. Martin H. Bertram, *Luther's Works*, vol. 30, *The Catholic Epistles* (Saint Louis: Concordia Publishing House, 1967), 4.

[3]This phrase was coined by John H. Elliott in order to describe the lack of scholarly attention given to 1 Peter in New Testament studies. See his "The Rehabilitation of an Exegetical Step-Child: 1 Peter in Recent Research," *JBL* 95 (1976): 243-54.

of scholarly interest in this New Testament text shows no sign of subsiding. In a sense, Petrine scholarship can be said to have come into its own within the last twenty years. No longer is 1 Peter merely seen as a Pauline prodigal, nor is it only clumped into the artificial (and somewhat dismissive) grouping known as "Catholic/General Epistles." Rather, commentaries, articles, and other studies have increasingly studied 1 Peter on its own merits as an expression of early Christian development.[4] In this sense, 1 Peter is being "rehabilitated" in academic circles.

Despite the continued rise of appreciation and attention given to 1 Peter, a scholarly consensus has not emerged on several issues in Petrine studies. Decisions on its date and authorship, for example, continue to elude exegetes. In closer relation to the issue addressed in this present study, the composition of 1 Peter has not been decisively determined by Petrine scholars. As will be demonstrated below, an enormous diversity of opinion has been attached to the genre, structure, integrity, rhetorical devices/goals, and compositional history of 1 Peter. Indeed, this state of affairs in Petrine studies functions as a formidable barrier to the ongoing process of studying this letter. Recently, two major contributions to the compositional issue have been produced. These two works will be discussed in some detail below.

This book is designed to answer the compositional questions, "How does the author of 1 Peter move the readers from one section of the letter to the next?" and, subsequently, "How does that transitional motion better inform us about the nature of this document?" This study will limit itself to the letter-opening (1:1-12), as it functions to set forth the rhetorical and compositional agenda for the rest of the letter.[5] We will begin this study with an overview of the history of

---

[4]See bibliography for a substantial listing of works that fit this tendency in Petrine studies. The most recent commentaries, for example, have been focused specifically upon 1 Peter itself, which is distinct from the older tendency to include 1 Peter in a volume dedicated to the "Catholic Epistles." Despite the continued rise of interest in 1 Peter, the annual SBL meetings still continue to include Petrine studies within the session "Hebrews and General Epistles." Evidently, Petrine studies will need to continue to increase in prominence before 1 Peter claims a place for its own in such meetings.

[5]The analysis of the letter-opening will also include a discussion of verses 13 and 14.

2

scholarship concerning 1 Peter's compositional design. This will be followed by delimiting the approach, which includes establishing the compositional framework within which this study will function, and an exegetical analysis of each of the major transitional passages of the letter-opening.

HISTORY OF SCHOLARSHIP

First Peter has received a great deal of attention in regard to compositional analysis.   Unfortunately, there are almost as many compositional theories on 1 Peter as there are Petrine scholars! It would appear that the literary nature of this document has remained an enigma. In his own compositional analysis of 1 Peter, Troy Martin offers one of the most comprehensive overviews of the history of scholarship on the compositional issue.[6]   Other compositional discussions of 1 Peter can be found in Ralph P. Martin's brief article on this issue, as well as in William J. Dalton's major work on 1 Peter.[7]

For R. P. Martin, the discussion centres around the *Sitz im Leben* of 1 Peter, specifically as articulated in the liturgical/baptismal hypotheses that dominated Petrine studies during the 1950s and 1960s. R. P. Martin briefly traces the various liturgical theories concerning 1 Peter, then argues for the unity of 1 Peter as a genuine epistle that has incorporated liturgical material into its epistolary form. He further argues that 1 Peter contains two baptismal homilies,

---

[6]Troy W. Martin, *Metaphor and Composition in 1 Peter*, SBLDS 131 (Atlanta, GA: Scholars Press, 1992), 3-39.

[7]Ralph P. Martin, "The Composition of 1 Peter in Recent Study," in his edited *Vox Evangelica: Biblical and Historical Essays* (London: Epworth Press, 1962), 29-42; William J. Dalton, *Christ's Proclamation to the Spirits*, Analecta Biblica 23 (Rome: Pontifical Biblical Institute, 1965), 62-91, 190-91. Beyond compositional discussions, there have also been surveys of scholarly and non-scholarly interpretations of specific themes or passages. Bo Reicke's *The Disobedient Spirits and Christian Baptism*, Acta Seminarii Neotestamentici Upsaliensis 13 (Kopenhagen: Einar Munksgaard, 1951) offers one notable example. In his study of 1 Peter 3:19 and 4:6, Reicke begins with an overview of some of the key interpretations of Christ's *descensus ad inferos*, ranging from the mid-second century up to the beginning of the 20th century (concluding with the interpolation theory). Of interest is J. W. C. Wand's ("The Lessons of First Peter: A Survey of Recent Interpretation," *Int* 9 [1955]: 387-99) overview of some key interpretations of 1 Peter, with a particular interest in the practical usage of these interpretations for pastoral work.

"one delivered before and the other after the rite."[8] In his more recent overview of 1 Peter, he reasserts his epistolary theory of 1 Peter, yet without the two homily aspect.[9] Although he takes into consideration some more recent compositional studies, specifically those of Schutter and Dalton, his overview of compositional discussions does not offer anything more than a cursory look at the field.

Dalton's discussion on compositional theories is far more extensive and valuable for Petrine studies. Dalton briefly outlines the development of the various partition theories, beginning with the homiletical hypothesis, as postulated by A. von Harnack, R. Perdelwitz, and W. Bornemann,[10] which broke with the traditional epistolary view of 1 Peter. This view argued that 1 Peter contained a sermon, running from 1:3-4:11 (5:11 for Harnack), which Perdelwitz argued was a baptismal homily. As sketched by Dalton, the homily theory was continued by Friedrich Hauck and H. Windisch, with H. Preisker developing Windisch's theory (in the third edition of the commentary) into an elaborate hypothesis that 1:3-4:11 was an actual baptismal liturgy, rather than a mere baptismal homily.[11] This line

---

[8]R. P. Martin, "The Composition of 1 Peter in Recent Study," 40.

[9]Andrew Chester and Ralph P. Martin, *The Theology of the Letters of James, Peter, and Jude*, New Testament Theology (Cambridge: Cambridge University Press, 1994), 87-133. According to R. P. Martin (who writes the sections on Jude, 1 Peter, and 2 Peter), the baptismal hypotheses of past scholarship have been disproved. He states at one point that, "as for the theories that arose out of an appreciation of the baptismal references and backgrounds -- the actual term baptism occurs only once at 3.21 in the text of 1 Peter -- the evidence is too scarce to support a primary designation of the document as a baptismal address. The traditional deposits (whether liturgical or homiletical) in 1 Peter which indicate a baptismal *Sitz im Leben* do not define the composition of the letter" (98-99). Furthermore, he states explicitly that "the more extreme theory based on what are claimed as baptismal materials, the baptismal liturgy theory, seems to have been totally disproved in the ongoing discussion of the nature of 1 Peter" (99).

[10]Dalton, *Christ's Proclamation to the Spirits*, 62-71. Dalton cites: A. von Harnack, *Die Chronologie der altchristlichen Literatur bis Eusebius* (Leipzig, 1897), 451; R. Perdelwitz *Die Mysterienreligion und das Problem des I Petrusbriefes*, Religionsgeschichtliche Versuche und Vorarbeiten XI.3 (Giessen, 1911); W. Bornemann, "Der erste Petrusbrief -- Eine Taufrede des Silvanus?" *ZNW* 19 (1920): 143-65.

[11]Friedrich Hauck, *Die Kirchenbriefe*, 8th ed, Das Neue Testament Deutsch 10 (Göttingen: Vandenhoeck & Ruprecht, 1957 [1936]), 36; Hans Windisch (and H. Preisker) *Die Katholischen Briefe*, Handbuch zum Neuen Testament 15, 3rd ed. (Tübingen, Kohr, 1951 [1911]).

of compositional thought continued with F. L. Cross and M. E. Boismard. Cross argued, primarily within an etymological study of πάσχω and πάθημα, that 1:3-4:11 functioned not only within a baptismal setting but specifically as an Easter baptismal liturgy/rite.[12] Boismard emphasized the role of hymnic material in 1 Peter, offering actual reconstructions of four hymns in 1 Peter. Rudolf Bultmann also had argued in 1947 for hymnic sources in 1 Peter.[13] Another significant partition theorist was F. W. Beare, who argued for the presence of liturgical fragments in 1 Peter. Beare further argued that 1 Peter 4:11-5:11 was added to the baptismal sermon when the presence of persecution became a present reality (whereas persecution was merely a possibility in 1:3-4:11, such as evidenced by the optative mood in 3:14).[14]

Having outlined these various compositional positions, all of which are developments from each other, Dalton then concentrates on refuting them in favour of seeing 1 Peter as a unified literary piece -- in essence a letter. Dalton recognizes the presence of liturgical, hymnic, and possibly even homiletical sources within the production of the letter, but argues that the text stands as a unified document within an epistolary form. Dalton then outlines his own compositional plan for 1 Peter, drawing on Albert Vanhoye's compositional devices as applied to Hebrews: inclusion, link-words, the announcement of important themes, repetition of key words, the change from statement to exhortation (or vice versa), and symmetry. To these devices Dalton further added the role of scriptural quotations.[15]

---

[12]F. L. Cross, *1 Peter: A Paschal Liturgy*, 2nd ed. (London: A. R. Mowbray, 1957).

[13]M. E. Boismard, *Quatre hymnes baptismales dans la première Épître de Pierre*, LD 30 (Paris: Cerf, 1961); Rudolf Bultmann, "Bekenntnis- und Liedfragmente im ersten Petrusbrief," *ConNT* 11 (1947): 1-14.

[14]See, however, Appendix 3 for an alternative reading of the optative in 3:14.

[15]Dalton, *Christ's Proclamation to the Spirits*, 72-86 (specifically 72-76); Albert Vanhoye, *La structure littéraire de l'Épître aux Hébreux*, Studia Neotestamentica 1 (Paris: Desclée de Brouwer, 1962).

The compositional histories supplied by R. P. Martin and Dalton are both limited to outlining the partition positions; consequently, they do not assist us in placing such positions within the broader stream of Petrine scholarship. This orientation is due to the particular agenda of both Dalton and R. P. Martin. R. P. Martin's hypothesis offers a refinement of the prevailing stream of scholarship of his day. Dalton, on the other hand, presents a strong polemical attack on the partitionists, which he uses to substantiate his apologetical defense of the epistolary unity of 1 Peter.[16] Furthermore, both are dated to a period when the homiletical/liturgical theorists dominated Petrine studies. Since the 1960s a great deal has transpired within the field. Specifically, a scholarly departure from partitional theories has occurred within Petrine studies. This is due in part to the decline in the *formgeschichliche* approach to the New Testament in favour of literary criticism, as well as the increased attention given to epistolary studies in general.[17]

When we turn our attention to Troy Martin's compositional history, we find a much more substantial sketch of Petrine scholarship. Martin traces six

---

[16]A similiar approach to Petrine scholarship is presented in James R. Slaughter, "The Dynamics of Marriage in 1 Peter 3:1-7" (Th.D. diss., Dallas Theological Seminary, 1992), 1-56.

[17]"Literary criticism" approaches texts as pieces of literature. Thus, the issues of genre, structure, key themes and rhetorical argumentation have been key concerns. Such an appreciation has typically resulted in viewing the text as a unified document. The concern over the literary nature of the document has, furthermore, resulted in a movement away from source critical and socio-historical concerns. Thus, literary critics, by and large, are not overly concerned with the transmission and redaction of source material. On a more technical note, several scholars have shown an interest in such literary motifs as "real author" (writer), "implied author" (writer), "implied audience," and "real audience." This literary motif has been most prominent within narrative analysis, though its applicability could easily be extended to other forms of literature. This book, however, does not adopt such technical literary perspectives on authorship and audience. Rather, 1 Peter's authorship and audience will be taken in the more typical view of "sender" and "receiver." A pseudepigraphal reading of 1 Peter, however, could lend itself to the "real - implied - implied - real" schema: The anonymous author = real author (1:1); the apostle Peter = implied author (1:1); the figurative description of the audience as God's "elect" in the "diaspora" (1:1) = implied audience; and the actual Christian community(ies) to whom the letter was sent = the real audience. For a brief study of 1 Peter from a modern literary critical perspective, see J. Davis McCaughey, "On Re-Reading 1 Peter," *AusBR* 31 (1983): 33-44. Although McCaughey does not specifically state the "real - implied - implied - real" schema, he does imply such a reading when he draws upon Ricoeur's theory of "play" and describes both "Peter" and the audience as "characters" in the document's literary strategy (38-39).

compositional "types" from antiquity to modern scholarship. He utilizes Urbanus Holzmeister's commentary as "the watershed between the older and the more recent scholarship."[18] Since Holzmeister's 1937 commentary, he argues, no new analytical "types" (approaches) to 1 Peter's composition have been developed. Rather, all modern scholarly approaches to 1 Peter have merely been adapted and developed versions of the six types.

The first "type" of compositional theory that Martin identifies is that illustrated by Pseudo-Euthalius. First Peter is seen as an instructional letter with no discernable compositional plan. Commentators of this type devise simple sectional headings to outline the basic themes in the letter, without considering the rationale behind the Petrine author's arrangement. This form of exegesis dominated ancient exegetes, and has even continued into modern scholarship.[19]

The second "type" of compositional theory focuses upon the change in audience within the text, such as the shift at 3:8 from specific groups to a general

---

[18]Martin, *Metaphor and Composition in 1 Peter*, 3 (full discussion of compositional history, pp. 3-39); Urbanus Holzmeister, *Commentarius in Epistulas SS. Petri et Judae Apostolorum*, Cursus Scripturae Sacrae (Paris: P. Lethielleux, 1937).

[19]Martin, *Metaphor and Composition in 1 Peter*, 4-5, 22-25. Some of the names attached to this type (as listed by Martin) are Pseudo-Euthalius ("Elenchus Capitum septem Epistolarum Catholicarum," in *Patrologia Graeca*, ed. J. P. Migne, vol. 85, 679-82); A. Jülicher (*Einleitung in das Neue Testament*, 7th ed, [Tübingen: J. C. B. Mohr (Paul Siebeck), 1931]); Walter Bauer (*Die Katholischen Briefe des Neuen Testaments*, Religionsgeschichtliche Volksbücher für die deutsche christliche Gegenwart 1.20 [Tübingen: J. C. B. Mohr (Paul Siebeck), 1910]); Hanns Lilje (*Die Petrusbriefe und der Judasbrief*, Bibelhilfe für die Gemeinde Neutestamentliche Reihe 14 [Kassel: J. G. Oncken, 1938]); Pietro De Ambroggi (*Le Epistole Cattoliche Di Giacomo, Pietro, Giovanni e Giuda*, La Sacra Biblia 14.1 [Torino: Marietti, 1947]); C. E. B. Cranfield (*The First Epistle of Peter* [London: S.C.M. Press, 1950]); Julian Prince Love ("The First Epistle of Peter"); Jean-Claude Margot (*Les Épîtres de Pierre* [Genève: Labor et Fides, 1960]); Alan M. Stibbs (*The First Epistle General of Peter*, The Tyndale New Testament Commentaries [Grand Rapids, MI: Eerdmans, 1959]); W. C. van Unnik ("Peter, First Letter of," in *The Interpreters Dictionary of the Bible*, vol. 3: *K-Q*, [New York, NY: Abingdon Press, 1962], 758-66); Roland De Pury (*Pierres vivantes* [Paris: Delachaux & Nestlé, 1944]); Eduard Schweizer (*Der erste Petrusbrief* [Zürich: Zwingli-Verlag, 1942]); Horst Balz and Wolfgang Schrage (*Die Katholischen Briefe*, Das Neue Testament Deutsch 10 [Göttingen: Vandenhoeck & Ruprecht, 1973]); and Norbert Brox (*Der erste Petrusbrief*, Evangelisch-katholischer Kommentar zum Neuen Testament 21 [Zürich: Benziger Verlag, 1979]). More recently, Peter Davids (*The First Epistle of Peter*, New International Commentary on the New Testament [Grand Rapids, MI.: Eerdmans, 1990]) has also stated that 1 Peter lacks a discernable compositional plan, and, therefore, "flows" together with each section naturally moving into the next.

admonition to all Christians. Pseudo-Oecumenius and Pseudo-Hilarius Arelatensis identified the compositional significance of the change in audience from general to specific in 1 Peter, yet it is the Venerable Bede (and subsequently Martinus Legionensis) who applied this method to the letter as a whole. Within modern scholarship, this method is applied primarily in regard to the subsections of the letter, rather than the major divisions. Furthermore, modern scholars have looked at the change from general to specific admonition, rather than general to specific audience.[20]

The third "type" of theory focuses upon the doctrinal and hortatory sections of the letter. This method began with Martin Luther, who divided the letter into two major sections: 1:3-25 (doctrinal teaching, which for Luther was the genuine and pure gospel) and 2:1-5:11 (exhortations based on the first section). This approach does utilize the second method, but only in regard to the subsections of the letter. Developments of this method placed a significant emphasis upon the use of indicatives and imperatives, which would thereby divide the letter between 1:3-12 and 1:13-5:11. The role of both doctrine and exhortation as compositional keys to the letter, however, has been shown to have methodological problems, and, therefore, this analytical method has not been a leading compositional theory in the field.[21]

---

[20]Martin, *Metaphor and Composition in 1 Peter*, 6-9, 25-26. Martin identifies the following with this type: Pseudo-Oecumenius ("Commentarii in epistolas catholicas," in *Patrologia Graeca*, ed. J. P. Migne, vol. 119, 509-78); Pseudo-Hilarius Arelatensis ("Exposito in epistolas catholicas," in *Patrologia Latina*, ed. J. P. Migne, Supplement 3, 83-106); The Venerable Bede (*The Commentary on the Seven Catholic Epistles of Bede the Venerable*, trans. David Hurst, Cistercian Studies Series 82 [Kalamazoo, MI.: Cistercian Publications, 1985]); Martinus Legionensis ("Expositio in epistolam I B. Petri apostoli," in *Patrologia Latina*, ed. J. P. Migne, vol. 209, 217-52); E. T. Mayerhoff (*Historische-critische Einleitung in die petrinischen Schriften* [Hamburg: Friedrich Perthes, 1835]); Georg Staffelbach (*Die Briefe der Apostel Jakobus und Judas, Petrus und Johannes* [Luzern: Räter & Cie, 1941]); Karl Reinhold Jachmann (*Commentar über die katholischen Briefe mit genauer Berücksichtigung der neuesten Auslegungen* [Leipzig: Johann Ambrosius Barth, 1838]); W. M. L. de Wette (*Die katholischen Briefe, griechisch, mit kurzem Commentar* [Halle: Eduard Anton, 1847]); Hermann Couard (*Die Briefe des Petrus, Judas und Johannes* [Postsdam: August Stein, 1895]).

[21]Martin, *Metaphor and Composition in 1 Peter*, 9-12, 26-27. Those whom Martin connects with this type are: Martin Luther ("Sermons on the First Epistle of Peter"); John Calvin (*Commentaries on the Catholic Epistles*, trans. John Owen [Grand Rapids, MI.: Eerdmans, 1948 (Edinburgh: T. Constable,

A fourth analytical "type" that Martin identifies was initiated by J. A. Bengel. In this case, thematic and literary considerations serve as the foundation for establishing the major compositional divisions. Bengel, for instance, established three major divisions along the thematic lines of the description of the readers. Of central importance for this compositional method is the rationale behind the structure of 1 Peter. This analytical approach has been popular in Petrine studies. Yet, as Martin articulates well in his critique, there are significant methodological difficulties with this type. Specifically, no consensus has yet emerged as to what constitute the controlling themes of the letter, nor how many divisions should be drawn. Although most exegetes have followed a three-part division, some have argued for four or five divisions. In regard to the number of divisions, the central point of debate revolves around 2:11-5:11, whereas 1:13-2:10 stands as a recognizable section among Petrine scholars.[22]

1855)]); Aretius Benedictus (*Commentarii in Domini nostri Jesu Christi Novum Testamentum* [Geneva: Petrum & Iacobum Chouet, 1607]); Nicolus Serarius (*Prolegomena Bibliaca et Commentaria in omnes Epistolas Canonicas* [Paris: Balthasar Lippius, 1612]); Johann Gerhard (*Commentarius super Priorem D. Petri Epistolam* [Hamburg: Zacharia Hertelius, 1709]); E. G. Selwyn (*The First Epistle of St. Peter* [London: Macmillan & Co., 1946]); Max-Alain Chevallier ("I Pierre 1/1 à 2/10: Structure littéraire et conséquences exégétiques," *RHPR* 51 [1971]: 129-42); Albert R. Jonsen ("The Moral Theology of the First Epistle of St. Peter," *ScEccl* 16 [1964]: 93-105); and Johann Michl (*De Katholischen Briefe*, Das Neue Testament 8.2 [Regensburg: Pustet, 1953]).

[22]Martin, *Metaphor and Composition in 1 Peter*, 12-17, 28-32. Martin identifies the following with this approach: J. A. Bengel (*Gnomon of the New Testament*, vol. 5, trans. Andrew Fausset [Edinburgh: T. & T. Clark, 1860]); Johannes Tobias Beck (*Erklärung der Briefe Petri* [Gütersloh: C. Bertelsmann, 1986]); J. C. W. Augusti (*Die Katholischen Briefe* [Lemgo: Meyersche Buchhandlung, 1801]); J. E. Huther (*Kritisch-exegetisches Handbuch über den 1. Brief des Petrus, den Brief des Judas und den 2. Brief des Petrus*, Kritisch-exegetischer Kommentar über das Neue Testament 12 [Göttingen: Vandenhoeck und Ruprecht, 1851]); Siegfried Goebel (*Die Briefe des Petrus, griechisch, mit kurzer Erklärung* [Gotha: Friedrich Andreas perthes, 1893]); Johann Martin Usteri (*Wissenschaftlicher und Praktischer Commentar über den ersten Petrusbrief* [Zürich: S. Hohr, 1887]); Ernst Kühl (*Die Briefe Petri und Judae*, Kristisch-exegetischer Kommentar über das Neue Testament 12, 5th ed. [Göttingen: Vandenhoeck & Ruprecht, 1887]); Julius Kögel (*Die Gedankeneinheit des Ersten Briefes Petri*, Beiträge zur Förderung christlicher Theologie 6 [Gütersloh: C. Bertelsmann, 1902]); Holzmeister (*Commentarius in Epistulas SS. Petri et Judae Apostolorum*); Peter Ketter (*Hebräerbrief, Jakobusbrief, Petrusbriefe, Judasbrief*, Die Heilige Schrift für das Leben erklärt 16.1 [Freiburg: Herder, 1950]); Eduard Lohse ("Paränese und Kerygma im 1. Petrusbrief," *ZNW* 45 [1954]: 68-89); A. M. Hunter and E. G. Homrighausen (*The Epistle of James, The First and Second Epistles of Peter, The First, Second, and Third Epistles of John, The Epistle of Jude, The Revelation of St. John the Divine*, The Interpreters Bible 12 [Nashville, TN: Abingdon, 1957]); Karl Hermann Schelkle (*Die Petrusbriefe. Der Judasbrief*, Herders Theologischer Kommentar zum Neuen Testament 13.2 [Freiburg: Herder, 1961]); Dalton

The fifth and sixth "types" of analytical methods utilized to determine 1 Peter's compositional structure are dealt with together by Martin: Type 5 advocates partition theories for understanding 1 Peter, and type 6 explores 1 Peter as liturgical in nature. Various homiletical and liturgical hypotheses have emerged from these types. These two methods have been outlined briefly above, and need not be rearticulated here. Suffice it to say that the form-critical method has had a significant impact upon Petrine studies (unlike in Pauline studies), surpassed only by the study of the Gospels. These methods have helped in unlocking some of the source material utilized by 1 Peter, yet do not offer a viable option for unlocking the compositional structure of the text. As Martin insists correctly, types 5 and 6 should be rejected due to the fanciful historical reconstructions upon which all their theories are based. The *Sitz im Leben* of 1 Peter is indeed important. Yet, the life-setting of the text can only be arrived at from an inductive analysis of the letter.[23] Close textual analysis is a necessary foundation for any

---

(*Christ's Proclamation to the Spirits*); Günther Schiwy (*Weg ins Neue Testament*, Kommentar und Material, vol. 4, Nachpaulinen [Würzburg: Echter-Verlag, 1970]); Leonard Goppelt (*A Commentary on 1 Peter*, trans. John E. Alsup [Grand Rapids, MI: Eerdmans, 1993]); Elliott (*A Home for the Homeless: A Sociological Exegesis of 1 Peter: Its Situation and Strategy* [Philadelphia, PA: Fortress Press, 1981]); David L. Balch (*Let Wives Be Submissive: The Domestic Code in 1 Peter*, SBLMS 26 [Chico, CA.: Scholars Press, 1981]); R. C. H. Lenski (*The Interpretation of the Epistles of St. Peter, St. John and St. Jude* [Columbus, OH: Lutheran Book concern, 1938]); M. E. Boismard ("Pierre (Première Epître de)," *Dictionnaire de la Bible*, Supplément 7: Pastorales-Pirot [Paris: Letouzey & Ané, 1966], 1415-55); Johannes Schneider (*Die Briefe des Jakobus, Petrus, Judas, und Johannes*, Das Neue Testament Deutsch 10 [Göttingen: Vandenhoeck & Ruprecht, 1961]); Ceslas Spicq (*Les Épitres de Saint Pierre*, SB [Paris: Libraire Lecoffre, 1966]); J. N. D. Kelly (*A Commentary on the Epistles of Peter and Jude*, Black's New Testament Commentaries [London: A. & C. Black, 1969]); Ernest Best (*1 Peter*, The New Century Bible Commentary [Grand Rapids, MI: Eerdmans, 1971]); Michl (*Die Katholischen Briefe*); David W. Kendall ("The Literary and Theological Function of 1 Peter 1:3-12," in *Perspectives on First Peter*, ed. Charles H. Talbert, NABPR Special Studies 9 [Macon, GA.: Mercer University Press, 1986], 103-20); Simon J. Kistemaker (*Exposition of the Epistles of Peter and of the Epistle of Jude*, New Testament Commentary [Grand Rapids, MI: Baker Book House, 1987]); H. J. B. Combrink ("The Structure of 1 Peter," *Neot* 9 [1975]: 34-63); and Jean Calloud and Francois Genuyt (*La Première Épître de Pierre: Analyse sémiotique*, LD 109 [Paris: Cerf, 1982]).

[23]Along the lines of source theories/partition theories for 1 Peter, W. Munro (*Authority in Paul and Peter. The Identification of a Pastoral Stratum in the Pauline Corpus and 1 Peter*, SNTSMS 45 [Cambridge: Cambridge University Press, 1983]) has argued that 1 Peter (along with Romans, Ephesians, Colossians, and the Pastoral Epistles) did not draw upon common material from earlier traditional sources. Rather, so argues Munro, there were extensive redactional activities in the first half of the second century, which resulted in a stratum which reflected a pro-Roman ideology. This

historical/community reconstructions. To reverse this procedure is methodologically suspect.[24]

Recently, two monumental works have been produced specifically addressing the compositional make-up of 1 Peter. Martin's *Metaphor and Composition in 1 Peter* (1992) has already been mentioned, and to this we will return shortly. The second major study is William L. Schutter's *Hermeneutic and Composition in 1 Peter* (1989). Both are helping to bring fresh attention to the issue of 1 Peter's compositional and rhetorical design.

Schutter's work originally appeared as a doctoral dissertation at Cambridge University in 1985, and was subsequently published in the WUNT series in 1989. It is devoted primarily to ascertaining the role of the Jewish scriptures in 1 Peter. Quotations and allusions to the scriptures are shown as playing a key role in the compositional development of 1 Peter. Schutter consequently argues that 1 Peter can best be understood as a homiletical midrash which hermeneutically follows pesher-exegesis (such as that found at Qumran). His thesis is illustrated primarily through a detailed discussion of 1:13-2:10, which he identifies as the body-

argument, which is based on highly speculative historical reconstructions (including dating, provenance, flow of influence, and so forth), has been refuted by J. H. L. Dijkman ("1 Peter: A Later Pastoral Stratum," *NTS* 33 [1987]: 265-71). Dijkman identifies a strong presence of Jewish traditions influencing 1 Peter to the extent that the Greco-Roman orientation argued by Munro does not suit the contents of the document. Although Dijkman's emphasis on the Jewish influence upon 1 Peter is overstated, it is important to realize that any interpretation of a document based upon conjectural historical reconstructions, such as Munro's, is only as strong as the quality of its reconstruction. In effect, one must be cautious of the dangers of subjectivity.

[24]Martin, *Metaphor and Composition in 1 Peter*, 17-21, 32-38. The proponents of these types have been dealt with above. A recent addition to this approach is William L. Schutter *(Hermeneutic and Composition in 1 Peter*, WUNT 2.30 [Tübingen: J. C. B. Mohr (Paul Siebeck), 1989]). Schutter refers to 1 Peter as a "Homilectic Midrash," specifically as illustrated by 1:13-2:10. More recently, Norman Hillyer *(1 and 2 Peter, Jude*, NIBC 16 [Peabody, MA.: Hendrickson, 1992]) has discarded not only the theory that 1 Peter is a baptismal liturgy, but even that 1 Peter has been modified from a liturgy. This is argued on the basis of desiring a unified theory of 1 Peter (6). Despite this claim, Hillyer draws heavily upon a liturgical understanding of 1 Peter throughout his commentary. Hillyer's thrust, however, is upon the dependence of 1 Peter on the Hebrew Bible (see for example 7-8). Consequently, although Hillyer should not be classified within type 5/6 technically, he does illustrate the influence that this approach has had upon Petrine studies -- including such conservative works as that produced by Hillyer.

opening. The hermeneutical *crux* for 1 Peter, according to Schutter, is 1:10-12.[25] An eschatological "history," where apocalyptic concerns emerge, seems to be the establishing premise for the hermeneutical enterprise of 1 Peter's use of Jewish scripture.

Schutter's approach to the structural design of 1 Peter is closely related to Dalton's methodology. Schutter devotes an extensive amount of his attention to establishing the various link-words, parallelisms, repetitions, and inclusio in 1 Peter, so as to ascertain the argumentative design of the letter. Noteworthy is his discussion of the transitional function of these compositional links. Compositionally, Schutter argues, 1 Peter breaks down as follows: prescript (1:1-2); blessing period (1:3-12); body-opening (1:13-2:10); body-middle (2:11-4:11), which divides into two major subsections (2:11-3:12/3:13-4:11); body-closing (4:12-5:11); and salutation (5:12-14).

Schutter's work makes a significant contribution in that he brings to scholarly attention the vital role that scripture (and hermeneutics) plays in the formation and argumentation of 1 Peter.[26] Yet in regard to compositional theory his proposal is unsatisfactory for a variety of reasons. First, his literary analysis is nothing more than an overextended development of Dalton's work.

---

[25]Schutter, *Hermeneutic and Composition in 1 Peter*, 85-166.

[26]A recent, albeit more modest, attempt at ascertaining and highlighting the significance of the Jewish scriptures in 1 Peter is Gregory R. Robertson, "The Use of Old Testament Quotations and Allusions in the First Epistle of Peter" (M.A. thesis, Anderson School of Theology, Anderson University, 1990). Robertson classifies the Petrine quotations and allusions into two functional catagories: (1) those dealing with relationships (the Christian's relationship with God, secular powers, and other Christians), and (2) encouragement. Surprisingly, Robertson does not cite Schutter's dissertation. Schutter's work is far more comprehensive and, thereby, offers a much more substantial analysis of 1 Peter's usage of scriptural sources. Robertson's two functional catagories, however, may prove useful in future research into Petrine scriptural source analysis. Another recent study of the Jewish scriptures in 1 Peter is W. Edward Glenny, "The Hermeneutics of the Use of the Old Testament in 1 Peter" (Ph.D. diss., Dallas Theological Seminary, 1987). Unlike Anderson, Glenny does indeed draw upon Schutter's work (and even offers several key criticisms of Schutter's hypothesis). On this issue of scriptural sources in 1 Peter, see also Klyne R. Snodgrass, "I Peter II. 1-10: Its Formation and Literary Affinities," *NTS* 24 (1977): 97-106. The ethical connotations of the Petrine author's use of Jewish scriptures has been highlighted by G. L. Green, "The Use of the Old Testament for Christian Ethics in 1 Peter," *TynBul* 41 (1990): 276-89.

Furthermore, Schutter's approach seems to force the text into a preconceived frame. Also, at times his interpretation of certain passages relies more on comparative analysis than inductive exegesis. This leads to seeing scriptural allusions and literary connections that may in fact not be present. Schutter's epistolary division of 1:13-2:10 as the "body-opening," furthermore, seems far too long for an opening. The same can be said of the body-closing. In regard to the claim that 1 Peter is a homiletical midrash, it is important to remember that the first century homily, as a genre, has not been adequately ascertained. Rather, all homiletical theories are based on either a comparison with homilies of a much later date, or are derived from a subjective understanding of what constituted an ancient homily. Thus, 1 Peter may indeed follow pesher-exegesis, but it should not be identified as a homiletical discourse. Finally, his approach does not appreciate the controlling themes of the text, nor how they interrelate with one another within the author's rhetorical strategy. For these reasons, Schutter's compositional theory is problematic, particularly in regard to the major structural outline that he marks out for us.[27] The enduring value of his work is in his understanding the Petrine author's appropriation of sources (specifically the Jewish scriptures), as well as his insightful exegetical observations, such as in the transition from 3:12 to 3:13 and the role of inclusion in the letter.

Troy Martin offers a landmark study in Petrine studies in regard to the question of composition. His work was originally accepted in 1990 as a doctoral dissertation by the University of Chicago and was subsequently published in the Society of Biblical Literature's dissertation series in 1992. Martin ascertains

---

[27]This is in contrast to Sharon Clark Pearson's strong support and utilization of Schutter's compositional theory. See Pearson, "The Christological Hymnic Pattern of 1 Peter" (Ph.D diss., Fuller Theological Seminary, 1993) -- specifically pp. 1-59, where she offers an overview of compositional theories on 1 Peter. She cites Martin (*Metaphor and Composition in 1 Peter*) in two extensive footnotes (p. 15, ftn. 1; p.16, ftn. 3), both of which only refer to Martin's six analytical types. Beyond this, she shows no evidence of interacting with Martin's thesis, nor even of offering a summary. This avoidance seems to be due to the close date between the 1992 publication of Martin's book and the 1993 acceptance of Pearson's dissertation (indeed, she is to be complimented for even showing any degree of awareness of and interaction with Martin's published thesis).

1 Peter's broad divisions by an extensive analysis of ancient epistolary conventions. Consequently, from a close inductive reading of the text, he establishes 1 Peter's breakdown as follows: prescript (1:1-2); blessing section (1:3-12); body-opening (1:13); body-middle (1:14-5:11); body-closing (5:12); greeting section (5:13-14a); and farewell (5:14b). Martin then turns his attention to ascertaining the compositional development of the body-middle, as epistolary conventions are unable to play a determinative role in this regard. He ascertains 1 Peter's literary genre as paraenesis. This is done by following Klaus Berger's two-fold criteria for paraenesis: (1) literary form and (2) social context (which includes social setting and social function).[28] In his study, Martin presents one of the most comprehensive overviews of ancient paraenesis yet to be produced. His command of the classical literature in his study further attests to this evaluation.

Having established the paraenetic nature of 1 Peter, Martin moves into the literary analysis proper of the body-middle. The significance of metaphorical constructions along certain thematic lines ("metaphor clusters") serves as the basis upon which the letter-body is constructed. At the outset, however, the description of the recipients serves as a foundational clue to the rhetorical strategy of the letter within its paraenetic agenda. The Christians addressed are described as the "elect strangers of the dispersion" in the prescript. This designation explains the ontological status of the addressees. All other metaphors in 1 Peter are generated by an overarching diaspora theme/metaphor. That is, the metaphor clusters of the letter body are derivative of the diaspora mentality or paradigmatic world view. Three metaphor clusters are highlighted by Martin, each of which has a general metaphorical theme that controls and collects the metaphors within each respective cluster: (1) 1:14-2:10 (The Οἶκος-Cluster, The Elect Household of God); (2) 2:11-3:12 (The Παρεπίδημος/πάροικος Cluster, Aliens in this world); and (3)

---

[28]Klaus Berger,"Hellenistische Gattungen im Neuen Testament," *ANRW* 25.2 (1984): 1033-1431; Martin, *Metaphor and Composition in 1 Peter*, 84-85. See also Leo Perdue, "Paraenesis and the Epistle of James," *ZNW* 72 (1981): 241-56.

3:13-5:11 (The Παθήματα Cluster, Sufferers of the Dispersion). The rhetorical goal of the Petrine author is to encourage the addressees to continue along their eschatological journey from "new birth" to their future "glory," and not to "defect" from the Christian faith due to opposition/suffering. In order to accomplish this task, the Petrine author employs a "rhetoric of suppression." That is, he emphasizes the positive aspects of their diaspora condition (i.e., their ontological relationship with the divine), and thereby "suppresses" the negative aspects of this condition.

Martin's compositional theory is the most promising proposal to date. He has highlighted the prominent role of metaphors in the letter, which is a key contribution to understanding the thematic flow of the document. Also, Martin's methodological rigor is noteworthy. He shows a strong sensitivity to the conventions of antiquity (including early Christianity) in letter writing and is careful not to read literary forms into 1 Peter that do not emerge from within the text. His inductive approach is a further strength of his thesis, especially given the analytical balance with other ancient texts. The unity of the document is further highlighted by Martin, as it was also by Schutter. With Martin, however, the thematic relations between the various sections of the letter, as well as the rhetorical rationale for these themes, are most clearly outlined and discussed. The role of the diaspora, as the controlling/generating metaphor, is an excellent contribution to Petrine studies, in that we are offered a socioreligious perspective by which the letter was both written and (probably) received. This diaspora mentality reflects the social condition/crisis of the addressees (as reflected in the letter), and thereby serves as a better occasion for the document than any hypothetically constructed *Sitz im Leben* developed by the partition theorists.

In regard to the controlling metaphor behind 1 Peter, Paul Achtemeier's 1989 article must be considered.[29] In discussing the role of figurative and literal

---

[29]Paul J. Achtemeier, "Newborn Babes and Living Stones: Literal and Figurative in 1 Peter," in *To Touch the Text: Biblical and Related Studies in Honor of Joseph A. Fitzmyer, S.J.*, ed. Maurya P. Horgan and Paul J. Kobelski (New York, NY: Crossroads, 1989), 207-36.

language in 1 Peter, Achtemeier argues that the Petrine author used the metaphor of "new people" as the controlling theme for the letter. This metaphor is used in 1 Peter in relation to "the chosen people of the OT, the people of Israel,"[30] so as to encourage the Petrine Christians -- as God took care of his "people" in the past, so he will now care for his "new people" in the present, and, thus, will care for this "new people" in the future. Achtemeier's study is closely in line with Martin's, even though the two emerged independently. In effect, Achtemeier's "new people" metaphor can be seen as similiar to the "diaspora" metaphor of Martin's work. Both emphasize the Petrine author's use of metaphorical language (drawn from Jewish self-perception), and see this language being adapted by the author to encourage and exhort a group of Christians facing some form of hostility (and, thus, a threat to remaining in their faith). Martin's "diaspora" metaphor, however, is a better designation than the "new people" metaphor, even though they are conceptually linked. The "diaspora" both incorporates and qualifies the "new people" theme. Diaspora more specifically identifies the sense of alienation and struggle, as well as eschatological hope, that characterize the Jewish people and their elect status ("peoplehood") before God. Consequently, "diaspora" serves well for understanding the nature of the ontological status of the Petrine community.

Methodologically, Martin's work is the most plausible compositional proposal to date, and deserves to be given its rightful place in Petrine studies. No serious literary analysis of 1 Peter can avoid taking this work into serious consideration. As a result, debate has already begun over certain features of his argument. Critics have been quick to jump on what has been perceived as an exaggerated usage of the diaspora as controlling metaphor.[31] For the most part,

---

[30]Achtemeier, "Newborn Babes and Living Stones," 235.

[31]Reviews of Martin's work that have appeared are Peter H. Davids (*CBQ* 55 [1993]: 594-95), J. Ramsey Michaels (*JBL* 112 [1993]: 358-60), Steven Richard Bechtler (*PrincSB* 14 [1993]: 81-83), and Casmir Bernas (*RSR* 19 [1993]: 265). Davids and Michaels are very positive in their evaluation, whereas Bechtler is quite negative. Bechtler's review, however, should not be given serious consideration, as the author clearly did not understand Martin's work, nor the issues and trends within Petrine scholarship. The issue of the diaspora is a key point of criticism in all three reviews,

such criticisms have been due to a misunderstanding of Martin's differentiation between general and specific metaphors as well as how metaphors interrelate with each other. Also, they have not understood what "diaspora," as a figurative designation of social perception and paradigmatic model, means. "Diaspora" was a key model by which the process of Jewish, then Christian, self-definition was accomplished in the exilic period onward. Eschatological hopes and restoration theology emerged from just such a designating perspective.[32] Consequently, Martin does need to articulate far more clearly the role of the diaspora in understanding the other metaphors. As the metaphor of the diaspora serves as the compositional device for unifying the three major sections of the letter-body, it would be helpful to ascertain the textual connections between these clusters so as to substantiate the unity of the letter. Martin only looks at the compositional transitions as transitional markers, to establish the beginning and end of sections and subsections, and as a result the transitional motion between the sections has not been fully addressed. Addressing this concern would help to substantiate both the unity of the document and the thematic relationship between the metaphorical themes of 1 Peter. Another criticism raised against Martin has been the need to

---

specifically Bechtler's which ignores the diaspora mentality behind 1 Peter, and even dismisses the third cluster's "sufferers of the diaspora" claiming that "1 Peter is drawing on *Christian* tradition [rather than Jewish] concerning the believer's suffering and glorification after the manner of Christ's. So it is not at all clear that the glue holding this third section to the first two is the diaspora metaphor" (83). Bechtler is in error on two counts: first, he does not recognize the *Jewish* nature of first/second century Christianity, and its appropriation of Jewish imagery to formulate specifically Christian identity; and second, he takes diaspora far too literally and narrowly. Bernas does not dialogue with Martin on the diaspora issue. Bernas' review, while seeing Martin's work as "solid" and deserving the attention of scholarship, merely criticizes Martin for being "boastful" (a criticism that all reviewers have noted) and lacking any "earth-shaking conclusion." Davids has offered the most balanced and insightful review of Martin's work to date.

[32] A reading of the Jewish sources of this period clearly reveals this diaspora-restoration theme. The whole concept of the diaspora as a temporary "alien" residence, as well as the hope of a restoration of the people of Israel, an "in gathering" back to the "land" of the covenantal promise, was central to the eschatological hopes of Jewish identity. A valuable survey of Jewish restorational hopes (as well as the Christian appropriation of Jewish restorational theology) can be found in Larry Murphy's "The Concept of the Twelve in Luke-Acts as a Key to the Lukan Perspective on the Restoration of Israel" (Ph.D. diss., Southern Baptist Theological Seminary, 1988).

do an in depth exegetical analysis of the letter so as to demonstrate more forcefully his compositional hypothesis.[33]

Having outlined the history of scholarship on the composition of 1 Peter, we are now ready to look at some methodological considerations for this present study. The historical survey has demonstrated the great diversity that exists in Petrine studies on this issue. A move away from liturgical/partition theories has been emerging in the field. With Dalton, Schutter, and Martin we are presented with a strong appreciation for 1 Peter's literary unity and style. The text has been increasingly studied as a piece of ancient (Christian) literature.[34] Martin's study has offered us with the most plausible compositional analysis of 1 Peter to date. A consensus on the composition of 1 Peter, however, is still wanting.

A RHETORICAL AND LITERARY APPROACH

The purpose of this present study is to ascertain the process of movement from one section of 1 Peter to another. Although the compositional transitions in this letter have been analyzed in regard to establishing the letter's structure, there has been little sustained analysis of the compositional transitional devices beyond merely being transitional markers. Schutter, as mentioned above, has been the closest study to date. Yet, even with his work the transitional motion in the letter is not a key point of analysis. Consequently, this present study proposes to look at the flow of movement within the letter.

This study emerges out of Martin's compositional theory. As already indicated above, compositional theories in Petrine studies are numerous and diverse. Martin's work has been selected as a working base for a variety of reasons. His study correctly identifies the genre of the letter as paraenetic.

---

[33]It is hoped that in his forthcoming commentary on 1 Peter, Martin will address this desideratum.

[34]Another recent study that argues for the importance of analyzing 1 Peter as literature is James R. Slaughter, "The Importance of Literary Argument for Understanding 1 Peter," *BSac* 152 (1995): 72-91. A key weakness in Slaughter's study, however, is his ignorance of Martin's literary study, which would have substantiated his argument far better than the heavy dependence on Schutter.

Furthermore, unlike several previous studies, his study appreciates 1 Peter's "letter" quality. By drawing upon ancient epistolary theory, Martin not only reaffirms the epistolary nature of 1 Peter, but he also offers a compositional explanation for sections of the letter previously identified. For example, the blessing-section (1:3-12) has been clearly identified in Petrine scholarship, but with varying understandings. Those who have postulated a liturgical and hymnic theory for this section of the letter have missed the most obvious explanation of its functional thrust, due to a failure to recognize the compositional role of ancient epistolary blessings, thanksgivings, and health-wishes. Consequently, Martin's study offers a compositional theory that best articulates the ancient practice of letter writing and, more importantly, the internal nature of the letter itself. Of special value is Martin's recognition of the role of metaphorical language within the letter. Consequently, Martin's study of 1 Peter offers the most plausible compositional framework within which to function.

Our own study is primarily literary in nature. First Peter is primarily an ancient early Christian piece of literature. It is not a theological creed that was meant to stand as a community rule for all time. Nor, for that matter, did the Petrine author intend to write "sacred scripture."[35] Rather, it was a letter written by a Christian leader in the name of Peter (who may have even been Peter) to a community of Christians facing a crisis of faith. The primary concern of the author was to encourage these Christians and to exhort them to continue their religious-eschatological journey. "Do not give up!" "Do not let your diaspora status result in a defection from the faith!" "Here's how to live in the world of

---

[35]Although the issue of inspiration and canonical criticism does not directly relate to this study, it is important to remember that 1 Peter (not to mention all the early Christian literature that we classify as "the New Testament") is an historical religious document that reflects a particular perspective of "gospel" message formulated to the needs of a specific community. The author most likely did not consciously intend to produce "sacred" text. Nor, for that matter, did the Petrine community receive 1 Peter as "scripture." Thus, the issue of inspiration is not to be discounted as pertaining to the document, but rather an authoritative canonical status must be removed from historical reconstructions of first and second century Christianity(ies), if we wish to enter into the mindset of the early Christians who produced and received these religious texts.

your exile!" This was the concern that the letter of 1 Peter addressed. It was a piece of literature written in response to a real situation involving real people. As the medium for communication was a literary type (a letter), the process of study must engage literary concerns.

Rhetorical Criticism and 1 Peter

Within Petrine studies, there have been several approaches taken in interpreting 1 Peter. Historical criticism has played a prominent role, primarily in regard to establishing the document's authorship, date, and historical setting. Source theories, primarily in regard to the reconstruction of hymns (specifically Boismard) and the incorporation of Jewish scriptures, have been closely aligned with liturgical studies. John H. Elliott and David Balch have been the foremost proponents for sociological methods being applied to 1 Peter.[36] Expositional and devotional interpretations of 1 Peter are obviously not lacking, and even continue to be produced.[37] Closely related to such approaches are theological debates, such as the issue of the early Christian "priesthood" (1 Peter 2), and the *descensus ad*

---

[36]Elliott, *A Home for the Homeless*; "1 Peter, Its Situation and Strategy: A Discussion with David Balch," (in *Perspectives on First Peter*, NABPR Special Studies 9, ed. Charles H. Talbert [Macon, GA: Mercer University Press, 1986], 61-78); Balch, *Let Wives Be Submissive*; *idem*, "Early Christian Criticism of Patriarchal Authority: 1 Peter 2:11-3:12," *USQR* 39 (1984): 161-73; "Hellenization/Acculturation in 1 Peter," (in *Perspectives on 1 Peter*, 79-101). These two scholars differ in their sociological presentation of the Petrine Christians. The two essays in *Perspectives on 1 Peter* cited above debate the differences. Whereas Balch sees the Petrine Christians in a process of acculturation with the Greco-Roman world, Elliott understands the sectarian nature of the Petrine Christians in a tension between intergroup relations and maintaining intragroup boundaries.

[37]Some fairly recent examples include Gordon H. Clark, *New Heavens, New Earth: A Commentary on First and Second Peter*, 2nd ed. (Jefferson, MD: The Trinity Foundation, 1993); Stuart Briscoe, *1 Peter: Holy Living in a Hostile World*, rev. ed. (Wheaton, IL: Shaw Publications, 1993 [1982]); and Fred B. Craddock, *First and Second Peter and Jude*, Westminster Bible Companion (Louisville, KY: Westminster/John Knox Press, 1995). The recent commentary by Donald G. Miller, *On This Rock: A Commentary on First Peter*, PTMS (Allison Park, PA: Pickwick Publications, 1993) pulls together scholarly work on 1 Peter for a lay audience.

inferos (1 Peter 3:18-20; 4:19). More recently, two key studies have been produced in regard to 1 Peter's ethical concerns and application.[38]

One method that has been underdeveloped in Petrine studies is rhetorical criticism. Although some studies have advocated rhetorical methods, no fully developed study of 1 Peter, to my knowledge, has emerged specifically devoted to an investigation of the rhetorical approach of the author of 1 Peter,[39] even though the Petrine author's rhetorical skills have long been recognized.[40] Martin's work is the closest to date, even though it is not explicitly presented as a

---

[38]Mary H. Schertz, "Nonretaliation and the Haustafeln in 1 Peter," in *The Love of Enemy and Nonretaliation in the New Testament*, Studies in Peace and Scripture, ed. William Swartley (Louisville, KY: Westminster/John Knox, 1992), 258-86; Kathleen E. Corley, "1 Peter," in *Searching the Scriptures*, vol. 2, *A Feminist Commentary*, ed. Elisabeth Schüssler Fiorenza (New York, NY: Crossroads, 1994), 349-60. Although both these studies are concerned with modern ethical issues, they differ in regard to their understanding of 1 Peter's Haustafeln. While Schertz sees 1 Peter advocating non-violence, and thereby offers substantiation for modern pacificist concerns, Corley interpretes 1 Peter as a violent text, specifically in regard to domestic violence (355-56). Corley contextualizes the Petrine Haustafeln within the contours of Balch's hypothesis. In conclusion, Corley views 1 Peter as oppressive for women: i.e., the letter does not advocate social change, but rather presents an exemplar of (christological) suffering which encourages the continuance of oppressive and violent social structures. Thus, according to Corley, 1 Peter should not be used for modern ethical (feminist) discussion (Cf. James R. Slaughter, "Submission of Wives (1 Pet. 3:1a) in the Context of 1 Peter," *BSac* 153 [1996]: 63-74; "Winning Unbelieving Husbands to Christ (1 Pet. 3:1b-4)," *BSac* 153 [1996]: 199-211; "Sarah as a Model for Christian Wives (1 Pet. 3:5-6)," *BSac* 153 [1996]: 357-65).

[39]Some examples are James W. Thompson, "The Rhetoric of 1 Peter," *ResQ* 36 (1994): 237-50; Lauri Thurén, *The Rhetorical Strategy of 1 Peter: with Special Regard to Ambiguous Expressions* (Åbo, Akademis Förlag, 1990); *Argument and Theology in 1 Peter: The Origins of Christian Paraenesis*, JSNTSuppl. 114 (Sheffield: Sheffield Academic Press, 1995); D. Ellul, "Un exemple de cheminement rhétorique: 1 Pierre," *RHPR* 70 (1990): 17-34; J. J. Janse van Rensburg, "The Use of Intersentence Relational Particles and Asyndeton in First Peter," *Neot* 24 (1990): 283-300; A. B. du Toit, "The Significance of Discourse Analysis for New Testament Interpretation and Translation: Introductory Remarks with Special Reference to 1 Peter 1:3-13," *Neot* 8 (1974): 54-79; and of course Martin, *Metaphor and Composition in 1 Peter*. Balch (*Let Wives be Submissive*) also shows an interest in the rhetorical strategy of the Petrine author, in regard to the domestic code. Pearson ("The Christological Hymnic Patter of 1 Peter") has shown some interest in the rhetorical aspects of 1 Peter, yet her interest is limited only to rhetorical *devices* and *syntactical structure*, rather than rhetorical *argument*. Also of some interest is Albert Wifstrand, "Stylistic Problems in the Epistles of James and Peter," *ST* 1 (1948): 170-82.

[40]F. W. Beare (*The First Epistle Peter* [Oxford: Basil Blackwell, 1958], 46-47), for example, has recognized the skilfullness of the Petrine author, and used this as an argument against Peter's authorship of the document. Cf. Goppelt (*A Commentary on 1 Peter*, 24): "The command of the language enables the author to utilize rhetorical devices of expression and to develop a sophisticated and memorable language form."

rhetorical study. Lauri Thurén's study of 1 Peter, although clearly stated as a rhetorical analysis, is limited merely to the participles which are considered ambiguous. Thus, Thurén's study is also not a comprehensive rhetorical critical analysis of 1 Peter.[41] The article by James Thompson, on the other hand, is

---

[41]Thurén's work (*The Rhetorical Strategy of 1 Peter*), furthermore, should be questioned as an acceptable rhetorical study based upon certain methodological bases. Specifically, his study of the participial phrases in 1 Peter does not properly contextualize the ambiguous expressions, but rather substantiates a participle's meaning on the premise of which rhetorical situation is being addressed. Methodologically, it would be more plausible to define the participle on the basis of the supporting syntactical context of the passage, and then to move toward the expression's rhetorical function. Another methodological problem is present in Thurén's delineation of the rhetorical situation of 1 Peter. He identifies a double implied audience in the text as follows: "As a circular letter sent to a diverse area, the text implies addressees, who have reacted in several ways to social pressure, the nature of which is also presumed to vary. I have characterized the two extremes as the 'active' and the 'passive' type of audience" (182). The "active response" refers to those addressees who would have reacted to social pressure by "improperly" responding which, according to the perspective of the implied author, "means improved social cohesion, but also loss of the contact with the non-Christians, so important for their missionary work" (182). The "passive response" is "instead assumed to be tempted to keep a low religious profile and assimilate to the non-Christian society in order to avoid further problems" (182). Based upon this highly speculative community reconstruction (which evidently reflects the actual community situation, rather than just the implied audience), Thurén compositionally divides 1 Peter so as to state the way certain rhetorical units would have interactively affected each of these two responses, with the ambiguous statements in 1 Peter functioning as rhetoric devices so as to address both rhetorical situations. This whole hypothesis is based upon such a speculative (and, thus, unsubstantiated) reading of the letter that it is clearly an implausible attempt at a rhetorical reading of 1 Peter. The tension between assimilation and sectarian withdrawal from society in the letter is better interpreted in sociological terms of maintaining community boundaries and, at the same time, remaining within acceptable parameters of the larger social setting. Thus, the tension between sectarianism and assimilation in 1 Peter reflects the realistic functioning of a religious community, rather than as a rhetorical situation of diverse responses to social pressure. In his most recent book, *Argument and Theology in 1 Peter: The Origins of Christian Paraenesis*, JSNTSuppl. 114 (Sheffield: Sheffield Academic Press, 1995), Thurén does focus upon the entire letter, but has not changed his basic position. This second book continues to depend upon modern rhetorical theory, rather than ancient rhetorical theory. Methodologically, it is best to work within the cultural context of the document, which means placing emphasis upon the ancient rhetoricians, and then to use the modern theories of argumentation, persuasion, and motivation as supportive devices in understanding the text. To reverse this emphasis, as Thurén has done, may remove the document from its sociocultural context and impose modern worldviews onto the text. Consequently, Thurén's approach to 1 Peter is not an appropriate rhetorical analysis of the letter. Thurén's study is useful in its call for rhetorical criticism to be applied to the study of 1 Peter, as well as for its emphasis upon viewing epistolography and rhetorical criticism as compatible in the study of ancient letters. Thurén's main contribution to Petrine studies has been to call scholars to consider seriously the rhetorical dimensions of 1 Peter. A better method in a comprehensive rhetorical study of 1 Peter would be to identify the role of *invention, arrangement, style, memory,* and *delivery* within the compositional development of 1 Peter. From this, a literary analysis of the text would identify the literary, or rhetorical, units to be studied. Here is where the epistolary and thematic (metaphorical) elements would come into play (i.e. the compositional arrangement offered by Martin). A syntactical study of each rhetorical unit would then be used to identify the stylistic attributes of the text. From this study, an assessment of the persuasive intention of the rhetorical unit

indeed a study of the rhetorical aspects of the whole of 1 Peter. Thompson's work, however, should not be considered a comprehensive rhetorical study. The brevity of the article, as well as the lack of appreciation for the epistolary nature of 1 Peter (he relies far to heavily on classical rhetorical theory, as applied to speeches, without properly considering 1 Peter as a letter in literary form), makes his work tantalizing at best. Given the current status of Petrine studies, it is a fair assessment to say that a rhetorical critical approach to 1 Peter is only now coming into being. The question still remains open as to what will, or will not, occur in Petrine studies in relation to rhetorical criticism. An example of a rhetorically oriented approach to 1 Peter can be found in John T. Demarest's commentary on 1 Peter, where he continually traces the various "motives" behind the actual text.[42] Demarest's study, given its date (1879), prior to the advent of rhetorical criticism proper, is to be signaled for showing such a serious concern for the persuasive approach adopted by the Petrine author. Yet, a fully developed rhetorical study of 1 Peter is still needed.

This present study is not specifically designed to meet this need in Petrine studies, but rather is designed to take the rhetorical strategy of 1 Peter into serious consideration. The transitional elements of a document are, however, elements of ancient rhetoric. That is, rhetoric, as a form of persuasive argumentation, seriously took the transitional flow of the discourse into consideration.

The elements of composition of concern in rhetorical handbooks apply well to 1 Peter. Within this study, we will primarily look at the rhetorical function of the transitional sections of the letter-opening. That is, while the Petrine author moves the reader from one section of the letter to the next, what persuasive goal

---

can be discerned, specifically in how the Petrine author moves the argument forward (which I refer to as *rhetorical motion*, a concept that includes the interactive relationship of the various compositional sections of the document). Such a step-by-step analysis of the letter would better articulate, inductively, the rhetorical strategy of 1 Peter.

[42]John T. Demarest, *Commentary on the Catholic Epistles* (New York, NY: Board of Publication of the Reformed Church in America, 1879).

is intended? This will be one of the questions that will be addressed in this study.
As Burton Mack has noted, the ancient rhetor would utilize a skeletal outline for
developing his/her argument, yet utilize various techniques so as to hide the
outline so as "to produce a composition that would appear to unfold naturally on
a given occasion."[43] In order to achieve this end, the rhetor's selection and use of
transitional devices was significant. Consequently, this present study is indebted
to the advances made in the development of rhetorical criticism -- yet it is not
strictly a rhetorical analysis in the technical sense. Hopefully, as an outgrowth of
this present work, a rhetorical analysis of 1 Peter will emerge in the future.

The development of a rhetorical argument is significant for understanding
1 Peter. Five basic elements, or stages of development, have been identified as
constituting the process by which a rhetor should build an argument.[44]

The first is "invention," or the collecting of data to support a thesis as well
as the conceptual process of establishing the thesis to be discussed. For 1 Peter,
the question of sources has been a highly controversial topic. The author clearly
drew upon the LXX, rather than the Hebrew Bible, both in direct citations and in
general allusions.[45] The Petrine author may also have drawn upon liturgical and
hymnic material. There is a great deal of debate as to what in 1 Peter can be

---

[43]Burton Mack, *Rhetoric and the New Testament*, Guides to Biblical Scholarship (Minneapolis,
MN: Fortress, 1990), 32.

[44]For a concise discussion of rhetorical criticism, see Mack's *Rhetoric and the New Testament*.
For his brief outline of these five stages, see esp. pp. 31-34. Also see George A. Kennedy's classical
work on rhetorical criticism in the New Testament, *New Testament Interpretation through Rhetorical
Criticism*, as well as his *Classical Rhetoric and Its Christian and Secular Tradition from Ancient to
Modern Times* (Chapel Hill, NC: The University of North Carolina Press, 1980), *The Art of Persuasion
in Greece* (Princeton, NJ: Princeton University Press, 1963), *The Art of Rhetoric in the Roman World*
(Princeton, NJ: Princeton University Press, 1972), and *Greek Rhetoric under Christian Emperors*
(Princeton, NJ: Princeton University Press, 1983). Mack's work, which offers one of the best concise
introductions to rhetorical criticism for the field of Christian origins, gives an extensive bibliography
of further works on rhetorical criticism, which would be far too comprehensive to list here.

[45]The role of the LXX, over against the Hebrew Bible, in 1 Peter is widely recognized in Petrine
studies. See for example, Selwyn, *The First Epistle of St. Peter*, 24-25; Werner Georg Kümmel,
Introduction to the New Testament, trans. A. J. Mattil, 14th rev. ed. (Nashville/New York: Abingdon,
1966), 297; J. N. D. Kelly, *A Commentary on the Epistles of Peter and Jude*, passim; Michaels, *1
Peter*, WBC 49 (Waco, TX: Word Books, 1988), xl-xli.

discerned as an early Christian hymn (or hymn fragment) and whether 1 Peter should be seen as a (baptismal) sermon or even possibly two sermons (with 4:11 being the dividing point and the prescript and closing of the letter merely being later additions). The theory of a liturgical *Sitz*, and genre, for 1 Peter has also been seriously postulated and considered in Petrine studies, as we have discussed above. Unfortunately, all such theories are highly suspect, due to being (1) based upon highly speculative and conjectural historical reconstructions of 1 Peter, and (2) unappreciative of the epistolary nature of the document. Still, the possibility remains that the Petrine author may have indeed utilized such material in the composition of the letter.[46]

The second element of compositional development is "arrangement." This element includes a basic outline for organizing the material collected. Various rhetorical arrangements could be drawn upon by a rhetor, yet personal ingenuity also would have played a role. It is in regard to arrangement that Martin's thesis has made the most substantial contribution for Petrine studies. The author of 1 Peter does not arbitrarily weave material together in a general and dispassionate manner. Rather, the author has carefully organized his material so as best to articulate the rhetorical strategy of the document. This is primarily based upon the author's creative utilization of metaphors, which are arranged according to carefully organized topoi. This process of arrangement is crafted according to the more general literary structure offered by epistolary conventions.[47] The compositional transitions in 1 Peter assist in interweaving this arrangement, so as to give the letter a more flowing and solid rhetorical thrust. It is with regard to these transitional movements with which our book is primarily concerned.

---

[46]A notable exception is Pearson, "The Christological Hymnic Pattern of 1 Peter," where she shows a strong sensitivity both to the epistolary nature of 1 Peter and to avoiding conjectural reconstructions.

[47]The epistolary genre has been identified as a literary form that functions as a framework for other literary genres. See Klaus Berger, "Hellenistische Gattungen im Neuen Testament," 1338 (cited by Martin, *Metaphor and Composition in 1 Peter*, 81).

The third element of composition is "style." The style of a particular rhetor is indicated in the selection and use of the grammatical tools of speech, including syntax and stylistic devices such as antithesis, paronomasia, parenthesis, epanophora, antistrophe, and reduplication. The issue of clarity of presentation also came into consideration, as did metaphorical devices. Early Christians, according to Mack, "were alert to the problems of style" and,

> in general, early Christian rhetoric was marked by unusual claims to authority, claims intended to enhance the privileged status and seriousness of the message even while creating imposing obstacles to its entertainment. Early Christians capitalized in this way on the novelty of their message and developed a number of styles that matched its sharp leading edge.[48]

In this regard, 1 Peter should be considered one of the most stylistically creative pieces of early Christian rhetoric,[49] specifically in the presentation of its paraenetic

---

[48]Mack, *Rhetoric and the New Testament*, 33.

[49]First Peter 2:10 offers a clear example of Petrine rhetorical style. This verse, which is at the transitional juncture into the second cluster, follows the rhetorical device of reduplication to interweave rhetorically synonymous and antithetical parallelism. The verse is divided into two primary clauses and two subordinant clauses as follows:

οἵ ποτε οὐ λαός --------------------- Primary Clause 1

νῦν δὲ λαὸς θεοῦ ---------------- Subordinate Clause 1

οἱ οὐκ ἠλεημένοι --------------------- Primary Clause 2

νῦν δὲ ἐλεηθέντες -------------- Subordinate Clause 2

As the above breakdown shows, the primary clauses are in synonymous parallelism, as they both articulate the past condition of the Petrine community, i.e. their outsider condition. The two subordinate clauses are also synonymously paralleled in that they both articulate the present "insider" condition of the Petrine community. The formation of these clauses presents the antithetical parallelism between Primary Clause 1 and Subordinate Clause 1 as well as Primary Clause 2 and Subordinate Clause 2. The relationship between the clauses is established through both syllabification (the two primary clauses containing six syllables, while the subordinant clauses, due to the length of ἐλεηθέντες, differ with a ratio of 4/6) and reduplication. Douglas A. Campbell (*The Rhetoric of Righteousness in Romans 3.21-26*, JSNTSuppl. 65 [Sheffield: JSOT Press, 1992], 93) defines this rhetorical device as follows: "These [cola and commata] are frequently connected through the repetition of key words, whether at the beginning, end, or throughout the clauses and phrases. If the initial word in successive statements is repeated, the technique is termed epanophora; if the last,

26

argumentation.[50] Martin best articulates this usage of paraenetical technique in
1 Peter, though other scholars have also recognized the significance of paraenesis
in the letter.[51] Martin's, however, is the most comprehensive study of Petrine
paraenesis to date, especially in exploring the relationship between paraenesis and
the other stylistic aspects of the author. The transitional devices used in 1 Peter
are stylistic in nature. Although conforming in some regards to general

---

antistrophe; and if one or more words are involved, reduplication." As shown in the breakdown,
repetition of key words indicates reduplication is being used to interrelate the four clauses. The bold
words are paralleled, with ποτε being elipsed in Primary Clause 2 (possibly to maintain the
syllabification of 6/6, or to merely make the sound more appealing to the ear). The underlined terms
are also paralleled (once again with elipsis being used [θεοῦ only appearing in Subordinate Clause
1 -- potentially to emphasis the elect status of being God's people in contrast with the community's
previous "non-elect" status of being a "no-people"]). Parallel are also the bold-underlined terms, and
the non-emphasized terms. The relational breakdown can be presented as follows:

οἵ ποτε οὐ		λαὸς
	νῦν δὲ	λαὸς θεοῦ
οἵ οὐκ		
		ἠλεημένοι
	νῦν δὲ	ἐλεηθέντες

The stylistic ingenuity of 2:10 (which is likely a scriptural allusion to Hosea 2) creates a balanced and
rhythmic presentation. In effect, the Petrine author has rearranged the material so as to raise the style
of the passage into a climactical conclusion to the first metaphor cluster. This verse emphasizes the
"insider" aspect of Christian election, specifically in contrast to the believer's former "outsider" status.
The opening of the second metaphor cluster (2:11) reverses this insider-outsider construct of 2:10 so
as to emphasize the "outsider" nature of the Petrine community within society. Thus, the antithetical
relationship between 2:10 and 2:11 emphasizes the perspective that the Petrine Christians are
"outsiders" within society, due to being "insiders" in God's realm. From this antithetical presentation
a sectarian mentality can be discerned within 1 Peter, yet with a level of social interaction with (the
non-Christian) society (as the second cluster articulates). This note is an expansion of a discussion of
the peace motif in 1 Peter; see Tite, "Pax, Peace and the New Testament," *Rel* 11 (1995): 307-09.

[50]The style of 1 Peter is taken by Best (*1 Peter*, 26-27) to support the unity of the letter, i.e. the
style is consistent so as to negate any postulations of two authors. Best cites Beare (*The First Epistle
of Peter*, 8) and E. Scharfe (*Die Petrinische Strömung der Neutestamentlichen Literatur* [Berlin, 1893],
3-22) in support of this observation.

[51]The classical essay on Petrine paraenesis is Eduard Lohse, "Paränese und Kerygma im 1.
Petrusbrief," [English translation, by John Steely, appears in *Perspectives on First Peter*, 37-59]. A
more recent addition to the study of Petrine paraenesis (specifically in regard to the *Haustafeln*) is
Hermann von Lips, "Die Haustafel als 'Topos' im Rahmen der urchristlichen Paränese: Beobachtungen
anhand des 1. Petrusbriefes und des Titusbriefes," *NTS* 40 (1994): 261-80.

conventions, the transitional devices in 1 Peter are best studied inductively, so as to ascertain their rhetorical function.[52]

Burton Mack, in articulating "memory," the fourth aspect of compositional development, states:

> *Memory* . . . referred to the process of memorizing the speech so that the delivery would be natural. Various techniques for doing this were devised, the most interesting being the imaginative creation of a scene in which vivid and striking images of persons, objects, and events would be set by association with the points, words, and figures of a speech one wished to remember.[53]

First Peter is especially notable in this regard. The imagery used in the letter creatively articulates the points of discussion in the document. It may indeed be that the Petrine author intended to use such "clustering" of images so as to enhance the memorization process for the assembly of Christians to whom the letter would eventually be read. Unlike an ancient speech, where the memorization process would be for the benefit of the speaker, a letter such as 1 Peter, which was read to an audience, may have used memorization techniques for the benefit of the community. This is one example of the differences between a rhetorical study of a speech and a rhetorical study of a letter.

The fifth and final element in the compositional process was "delivery" of the work. In our book the primary concern is with the literary aspects of 1 Peter, rather than its oral presentation. Yet, the role of "personation" in delivery may assist us in understanding the rhetorical function of the apostolic claims of 1:1 (especially in relation to 5:1, 12-13), if indeed the document is pseudepigraphical. To present the letter in the name of "Peter" would have given its reception the rhetorical flavour of a situational setting with which the Petrine community could

---

[52]As I have already indicated, this is a key weakness in Schutter's hermeneutical study of 1 Peter's compositional devices. Although Schutter is correct in identifying the presence of these devices in 1 Peter, Martin (*Metaphor and Composition in 1 Peter*, 138-39) is somewhat justified in arguing that the transitional devices in 1 Peter need to be identified internally (especially given the paraenetic nature of the body-middle).

[53]Mack, *Rhetoric and the New Testament*, 34; *Rhetorica Ad Herennuim* 3.16.28-24.40.

relate -- i.e. the martyrdom of this famed apostle under the persecution of Nero. The significance of "apostle of Jesus Christ" in 1:1 for such a rhetorical function is well stated by Lenski, who advocates Peter's authorship. Lenski says:

> The brief apposition: "apostle of Jesus Christ" . . . states in what capacity Peter writes, namely as one commissioned by Jesus Christ. The motive for writing as well as the purpose of writing are combined. The readers will be ready to hear and heed what Christ's apostle feels impelled to say to them.[54]

The rhetorical value of using "Peter" to encourage righteous sufferers is evident within the Peter tradition, as evidenced in *1 Clement* 5:4, which also emerged from Roman Christianity most likely about the same time as 1 Peter:

> Peter, who because of unrighteous jealousy suffered not one or two but many trials, and having thus given his testimony went to the glorious place that was his due.[55]

Such a view of Peter, as a righteous sufferer who attained a heavenly glory, would fit well with the rhetorical strategy of 1 Peter. This emerges in the letter most prominently with a christological typology of suffering/glory in 3:18-4:1.[56] Thus, a Petrine type may have been deemed of value for the hortatory and consolatory intentions of the Petrine author. Consequently, even the opening prescript would have been modified so as to enhance the rhetorical strategy of 1 Peter.

Historical-Critical Concerns

In regard to historical issues within Petrine studies, a brief comment should be made. A demarcation seems to have emerged between scholars doing "historical critical" work and those doing "rhetorical critical" work. I wish briefly

---

[54]Lenski, *Interpretation*, 20. Unless otherwise stated, all translations from the Bible are taken from the NRSV.

[55]Translation is Kirsopp Lake's, *Apostolic Fathers*, LCL, 1:17.

[56]See Appendix 3 below.

to outline my own views on the historical setting of 1 Peter, specifically in regard to the rhetorical nature of the text.

The terms used in this study to refer to the addressees of 1 Peter, such as "Petrine community" and "recipients," do not intend to postulate the idea of a single community to which the letter was written. The general nature of the letter, in addition to the five provinces mentioned at 1:1 ("Pontus, Galatia, Cappadocia, Asia, and Bithynia"), suggests that the author of 1 Peter intended to write an encyclical letter to Christians in Asia Minor. This understanding of 1 Peter has pervaded Petrine studies. For our study, we use the term "Petrine community" merely to refer to the recipients of 1 Peter without any specific historical designation. Indeed, the community addressed may well have been a singular community. Given the metaphorical significance of the diaspora metaphor in 1:1-2 (specifically the description of the recipients in 1:1 as "exiles" and the "dispersion") and 5:13 ("Babylon" -- which is best taken as a cryptic term for Rome),[57] it is plausible to understand the five provinces as merely a reference to the community's diaspora status, rather than as a sociological description of the community itself. Thus, with a metaphorical understanding of the letter kept in mind, the recipients of 1 Peter may not have been spread out over five provincial territories of Asia Minor. Regardless of how one wishes to understand the five provinces in 1 Peter, this present study utilizes the term "Petrine community" in a general and non-specific sense.[58]

---

[57]First Peter is best seen as a part of "Roman Christianity," regardless of whether it is authentic or not, and whether it reflects an earlier stage of development of the Roman congregation (60s C.E.) or a later stage of development (110s C.E.). Walter Bauer was probably correct in associating 1 Peter, which he understood as being composed near the end of the first century, with the expansion of Roman influence over other congregations (See Bauer, *Orthodoxy and Heresy in Earliest Christianity* trans. Robert A. Kraft and Gerhard Krodel [Philadelphia, PA: Fortress Press, 1971 (1934)], 122-21 128).

[58]Furthermore, there is no need to postulate a "Petrine school," such as advocated by Ernst Bes (*1 Peter*, New Century Bible [London: Oliphants, 1971], 64-65), which produced material in the nam of Peter after the apostle's death. No evidence exist for the existence of any circle of Peter's disciple in Rome or elsewhere. David Henry Schmidt ("The Peter Writings: Their Redactors and The Relationships" [Ph.D. diss., Northwestern University (Evanston, IL), 1972]) has convincingl

Closely connected to the issue of 1 Peter's historical setting is the usage of metaphors. Martin's recognition of the role of metaphorical language within the letter is one of his key contributions to Petrine studies. In any attempt to "read through" the text in order to ascertain the historical setting of the letter, historians must seriously contend with the religious language incorporated into 1 Peter. Errors have arisen when sociological analysis has read far too literally into key terms and phrases, without appreciating the difficulty of using metaphorical language/imagery.[59] By its very nature, metaphors elude clarity. Nevertheless their functional purpose in a document is clear.[60]

---

established that no connection exists between the various "Petrine writings" that validates any hypothesis of a Petrine corpus (such as we have in the Pauline tradition), nor any school behind these diverse documents. Instead of a Petrine *school* or *corpus*, I would contend that it is more plausible to speak of a Petrine *tradition*, where the characterization of "Peter" within various early Christian communities would have occurred. Thus, Peter was appropriated by different Christians, who saw him as "their own" exemplar (pro or con). This perspective on Peter is similiar to the appropriation of "Paul" within such second century groups as the Valentinians and the Marcionites. No actual connection is necessary for such appropriation of Peter; thus, a "tradition" best serves as a description of the dynamics of Peter in 1 Peter, rather than a "Petrine school."

[59]This is the primary weakness of Elliott's *A Home for the Homeless*. For example, Elliott is correct in his sociopolitical discussion of the technical (secular) use of the terms παρεπίδημος and πάροικος (21-58), yet he has not recognized the figurative dimensions that such terms can take when appropriated by an author, especially within a religious context. Instead, Elliott has taken these terms as literal designations for the status of the Petrine Christians' social status prior to conversion. Indeed, he goes so far as to argue for a rural social setting based largely upon these terms. In contrast to Elliott's social history of 1 Peter, it is more persuasive to see these terms being used for articulating social perception rather than social description. Elliott interprets terminology analogically, rather than using literary context and social models to identify the rhetorical strategy of the text. Elliott draws lines of connection between specific terms without any clear substantiation. Thus, the plausibility of his social-exegetical analysis of 1 Peter is lessened. Furthermore, Achtemeier ("Newborn Babes and Living Stones" 212-13) has helped to emphasize the interplay of both literal and figurative language in 1 Peter. Best's (*1 Peter*, 16-17) brief outline of the sociological and religious context of the Petrine community, albeit briefer, is far more constructive.

[60]See Mary R. Lifkowitz, "Metaphor and Simile in Ennius," *CJ* 55 (1959): 124: "These are not complete images, but separate metaphorical terms, superimposed upon one another, each term having its own particular emphasis. By using this metaphorical vocabulary, the poet says in a few words what the prose writer would take many to express. Ennius' descriptive metaphors are not merely decorative. They are emphatic. By means of metaphor the poet brings out one particular aspect of an action or thing." As Lefkowitz illustrates, metaphors are significant when used (and, thereby, function) to convey the message of the text in a brief and vivid fashion. Metaphorical language is not decorative or secondary. This same principle should also be applied to the function of metaphorical language in 1 Peter.

Specifically, the diaspora metaphor, which functions as the overarching metaphor that generates and controls the others, perhaps best articulates the social understanding of the Petrine community. The recipients of 1 Peter appear to have had a particular self-image of themselves in light of their socioreligious condition. This condition was one of isolation and (perceived or actual) persecution. It is not important whether an actual form of persecution occurred or not. Rather, it is the community's understanding of estrangement that is important. Indeed, it is possible that no real suffering was facing the community. Their suffering may have been one of social perception, rather than actual social condition. For the Petrine community, however, this would have made no difference; the suffering was real to them. Thus, the Petrine author must address the concerns of a community "in crisis." Consequently, even if a real manifestation of persecution did face the community, the specific type of persecution (imperial, local, social, potential or present reality) is not important for our present study. The issue of persecution has dominated Petrine studies far too long in the search for the answers to such historical issues as date and authorship, while not recognizing the role that the concept of persecution played in the molding of the self-understanding of the Petrine community.[61] That is, how did the readers of 1 Peter understand themselves? What was their process of religious self-understanding? How did the author of 1 Peter respond to the dynamics being played out in the community? Although not all of these questions can be fully answered in this present study, they do frame the conceptual basis for this work. A metaphorical reading of 1 Peter opens the document for a thorough understanding of the social dynamics of the Christians addressed in the letter, beyond the more surface level questions of date, authorship, and location.

---

[61]Best, *1 Peter*, 42 states the futility of using the theme of persecution to date the text, when he says: "We may note finally that since the references to persecution are not sufficiently definite to permit us to connect them with any known period of persecution and since they do not relate particularly to state action against Christians they are of little assistance in the determination of the date of 1 Peter."

In regard to date and authorship, little can be said with any certainty. The arguments over this issue are solid on both sides when it comes to accepting or rejecting Peter's authorship. Yet, despite extensive attempts to prove or disprove Peter's authorship of the letter, or, for that matter, to ascertain the role of Silvanus in the composition of the letter, no consensus has emerged, and it is unlikely that any consensus will emerge in the near future. The issue of authenticity is best left aside as unresolved and unresolvable.

This present study is a literary study of 1 Peter, yet this should not be taken to imply an ahistorical perspective. The role of historical criticism, especially with the continued appreciation for sociological methods, needs to be applied to 1 Peter even more vigorously than ever. Within certain circles, however, a demarcation has occurred between literary critics and historio-critical scholars.[62] It is not the intent of this study to praise one form of scholarship over another. The interpretation of ancient texts is best served by a correlative approach that utilizes a variety of methods and sources. This call for a "multiple method" approach in Christian origins is most applicable to the study of narratives (primarily the four New Testament gospels). Yet, this call should also be raised for epistolary studies, especially with the continued rise of rhetorical criticism, as well as the significance of structuralism in the study of texts. The beginning point for any historical or socioreligious study of a text, however, must be a literary understanding of the document (*Formkritik* and *Gattungsgeschichte*). It is hoped that this book will assist in setting down the literary foundation for such historical analyses of 1 Peter.

---

[62] For a useful overview of the so-called "New Criticism," its impact, and the division between intrinsic methods and extrinsic methods, see Robert Detweiler, "After the New Criticism: Contemporary Methods of Literary Interpretation," in *Orientation and Disorientation: Studies Presented in Honor of William A. Beardslee*, ed. Richard J. Spencer, PTMS 35 (Pittsburgh, PA: The Pickwick Press, 1980), 3-23; and Charles T. Davis, "A Multidimensional Criticism of the Gospels," *ibid*, 87-98 (esp. 89). Also of importance for understanding such literary methods and New Testament studies, see Norman R. Petersen, "Literary Criticism in Biblical Studies," *Orientation and Disorientation*, 25-50; and Edgar V. McKnight, "The Contours and Methods of Literary Criticism," *Orientation and Disorientation*, 53-69.

The procedure that will be followed in this book will be to isolate the key transitional passages of 1 Peter's letter-opening, and then to exegete them accordingly. By utilizing Martin's compositional theory, the major transitional sections of 1 Peter, including the letter-opening, will have already been determined.[63] This book will study the transition from one section of the letter-opening to the next, through a variety of literary tools (grammatical, rhetorical, and so forth), as the context allows. The exegesis will be placed within the broader context of the literary function of the compositional units being studied. Thus, an extended discussion of such compositional units as the Petrine prescript will be offered to answer the more specific question being asked. The compositional movement within 1 Peter, furthermore, promises to offer various insights into key issues within Petrine studies. These will be addressed after the exegesis proper of 1 Peter. Due to the space restraints, this book will limit itself to an analysis of the major compositional transitions in the letter-opening. Several scholars, including Dalton, Martin, Schutter, and Thurén, have already dealt with the minor breaks in their respective works. There is no need to reiterate their conclusions.

---

[63]The only transition within a cluster that will be dealt with significantly, however, is the division of the two subsections of the first metaphor cluster, where I modify Martin's division at 2:1. As this discussion is somewhat peripheral it is presented in Appendix 1 (cf. Appendix 2). Beyond this one transition, I will confine myself primarily to the major breaks in the text.

CHAPTER TWO:
LETTER-OPENING

INTRODUCTION

This chapter addresses the exegesis proper of the compositional transitions of 1 Peter's letter-opening (1:1-12).[1] The opening sections of the letter will be discussed, beginning with the prescript's movement into the blessing-section (1:2-3). The transition from the blessing to the body-opening (1:10-13) will then be discussed. The final transition to be addressed will be from the body-opening to the body-middle (1:13-14). In the discussion of the prescript, a somewhat extended analysis of the literary nature and purpose of ancient prescripts, specifically how they relate to the Petrine prescript, will be outlined. As this compositional unit is so small, yet so vital to the programmatical thrust of the letter, it must be dealt with in some detail.

THE NATURE OF THE PRESCRIPT (1:1-2)[2]

The first compositional unit within 1 Peter is the prescript, which functions to establish the relationship of the sender and the addressee:[3]

Πέτρος ἀπόστολος Ἰησοῦ Χριστοῦ ἐκλεκτοῖς παρεπιδήμοις διασπορᾶς Πόντου, Γαλατίας, Καππαδοκίας, Ἀσίας καὶ Βιθυνίας, κατὰ πρόγνωσιν θεοῦ πατρὸς ἐν ἁγιασμῷ πνεύματος εἰς ὑπακοὴν καὶ ῥαντισμὸν αἵματος Ἰησοῦ Χριστοῦ, χάρις ὑμῖν καὶ εἰρήνη πληθυνθείη. (UBS 4th ed.)

Peter, an apostle of Jesus Christ, to elect visitors of a diaspora comprising of Pontus, Galatia, Cappadocia, Asia and Bithynia,

---

[1]For the sake of this study, I am using the designation "letter-opening" to refer to the introductory sections of 1 Peter, which constitutes the prescript and the blessing. An inclusion of the body-opening is also necessary for this study so as fully to ascertain the transitional motion within the letter-opening.

[2]Part of the following appeared in an article entitled "The Compositional Function of the Petrine Prescript: A Look at 1 Peter 1:1-3," *JETS* 39 (1996): 47-56.

[3]John L. White, *Light from Ancient Letters* (Philadelphia, PA: Fortress Press, 1986), 198.

according to father-god's foreknowledge through a holy spirit for obedience and sprinkling of Jesus Christ's blood, may grace and peace be multiplied to you. (my translation)

As will be demonstrated below, the Petrine prescript functions as the programmatical introduction for the entirety of 1 Peter. Consequently, a clear understanding of the nature of the prescript is needed in order to ascertain the rhetorical strategy of 1 Peter. From a discussion on the nature of prescripts the rhetorical function of the transitional sections of 1 Peter will more clearly emerge.

Ancient letter prescripts followed a specific stylized form. As Francis Xavier J. Exler has noted, the basic opening formula was "From A to B, Greeting (χαίρειν)."[4] This formula has been identified in ancient Greek letters running from the third century B.C.E. to the third century C.E.. Similarly, the prescripts in the Aramaic letters studied by Fitzmyer also exhibit this same formulaic style.[5] Exler also noted the variations that developed from this standard formula. The addition of qualifying phrases, such as πολλά, τῷ πατρί, ἀδελφῷ, extended the opening formula so as to add clarity and enhance the relational connection between the sender and the addressee. Changes in the formula's structure also have been observed. For example, the A to B greeting has been changed to "To B from A, greeting," "To B from A,""To B, greeting, A," "From A," "A to B," "To B."[6] Another interesting change in the opening formula was the addition of

---

[4]Francis Xavier J. Exler, *The Form of the Ancient Greek Letter: A Study of Greek Epistolography* (Washington, D.C.: Catholic University of America, 1923), 23.

[5]Joseph A. Fitzmyer, "Some Notes on Aramaic Epistolography," *JBL* 95 (1974): 211-13.

[6]Fitzmyer ("Some Notes on Aramaic Epistolography," 211-13) has recognized similar variations within Aramaic letters. He identifies five basic formulaic variances (211) -- "The *praescriptio* when it is not simply implied, is usually expressed in one of five ways: (i) 'To X, your servant/brother/son, (greeting)'; (ii) 'To X, from Y, (greeting)'; (iii) 'From X, to Y, (greeting)'; (iv) 'X to Y, (greeting)'; (v) 'To X, (greeting)'." The significance of a study of Aramaic letters for understanding early Christian letters is briefly suggested by Fitzmyer (202): "In a sense this inquiry forms but another aspect of the generic problems of the Aramaic background of NT writings, or more properly of Aramaic interference in NT Greek. . . . Furthermore, J. N. Sevenster has raised a question about the Palestinian origin of James and 1 Peter in a new way, and in the light of it one could ask about the influence of Aramaic epistolography on such letters." Also see Chan-Hie Kim (*Form and Structure of the Familiar Greek Letter of Recommendation*, SBLDS 4 [Missoula, MT: University of Montana, 1972]), who notes the

a "health wish" (ἐρρῶσθαι or ὑγιαίνειν). Among Aramaic letters, specifically those found as ostraca, the brevity of a letter resulted in the mixing of the greeting and the prescript.[7] The rarer opening of the optative or imperative (χαίροις or χαῖρε) is also found. Although it has been postulated that this rare form was the one that slaves primarily would use, Exler has convincingly refuted such a claim.[8] What is important to note is that the prescripts grew in complexity in order to establish relational feelings between the sending and receiving parties. Furthermore, the extensions played a key role, in many cases, in establishing the letter's specific agenda. Within early Christian letters the prescript establishes both the relational connection between the reader and the author,[9] as well as the letter's conceptual thrust. According to J. Ramsey Michaels, the prescript served a theological-functional purpose, so as to set the stage for the rest of the letter.[10]

---

same literary tendency. Kim utilizes more recent source material, and therefore is an important addition to Exler's older study. Kim's study is not critical for our purposes since he is interested in the Greek "letter of recommendation" (a genre to which 1 Peter does not belong, unlike Philemon, which is a letter of recommendation; See Kim, *Form and Structure*, 123; A. J. Malherbe, "Ancient Epistolary Theory," *Ohio Journal of Religious Studies* 5 [1977]: 63-71; cf. Allen Dwight Callahan, "Paul's Epistle to Philemon: Toward an Alternative *Argumentum*," *HTR* 86 [1993]: 357-76). Another useful overview of Greek epistolography is M. Luther Stirewalt, Jr., *Studies in Ancient Greek Epistolography* (SBL Resources for Biblical Study 27 [Atlanta, GA.: Scholars Press, 1993]).

[7]Fitzmyer ("Some Notes on Aramaic Epistolography," 213): "On the ostraca one finds, undoubtedly because of the brevity of the message, an opening that mixes greeting and *praescriptio*."

[8]The prior position was argued by F. Ziemann, *De Epistularum Graecarum Formulis Sollemnibus Quaestiones Selectae* (Berlin: Haas, 1912), 296. Exler cites and refutes Ziemann's position in *The Form of the Ancient Greek Letter*, 68.

[9]Martin (*Metaphor and Composition in 1 Peter*, 43) clearly states the functional aspect of the Petrine prescript along these lines: "The identification of the writer as an apostle definitely establishes a particular relationship between him and the reader of the letter. Whether or not the writer is indeed an apostle or even truly Peter, the letter makes this claim and establishes this relationship."

[10]J. Ramsey Michaels (*1 Peter*, 4) identifies 1 Peter as a encyclical "diaspora letter" -- in comparison to James 1:1; Revelation 1:11; Jeremiah 29:4-23; *2 Apocalypse Baruch* 78-87; 2 Maccabees 1:1-10a, 10b--2:18; Acts 15:23-29. Michaels perceives 1 Peter as such a letter addressed to Gentile Christians within the five Roman provinces listed in the prescript. Michaels declares the function of the prescript in 1 Peter as follows (13-14):

The function of the epistolary introduction is to identify the recipients of the letter as God's chosen people living as strangers in the diaspora and to lay a theological

In establishing the conceptual direction of the letter, 1 Peter's prescript sets forth the diaspora theme for the entire letter at the very outset.[11] As Norman Hillyer observes, the author "describes the readers in three ways": as "God's elect," "strangers in the world," and "scattered throughout."[12] Each of these designations identifies the recipients of the letter, within the thematic framework of the text.[13] That is, the author uses the epistolary formula of the prescript to present the self-identification of the Petrine community.

Compositionally, the prescript has been identified as a summation of the major sections of the letter. Heinrich Rendtorff, as cited by Martin, has stated that 1:1-2 encapsulates the letter's concern for the elect strangers, whose homelessness is due to their destiny with God.[14] Troy Martin, following Rendtorff's lead, has

---

basis for their identity. This theological basis extends only as far as their baptism. All that Peter knows of them is that they are communities of baptized Christians and consequently, like the Jews, "strangers" to the cities and provinces where they live. Not a clue has yet been dropped that their estrangement means suffering for them or that their baptism has given them hope of vindication. As Peter holds out to them grace; and peace, the issues to be addressed in his epistle have not even been raised, yet the resources for addressing those issues -- the redemptive work of God through Christ, and the resultant character of the community thus redeemed -- are already in place.

Also of interest, in regard to thematic analysis of the prescript, is Francis H. Agnew's treatment of the theme of obedience in 1 Peter 1:2b ("1 Peter 1:2 -- An Alternative Translation," *CBQ* 45 [1983]: 68-73).

[11]Similarly, Paul's epistolary prescript in Galatians 1:1 sets "the direction of the subsequent argumentation" and thus "Paul's self-presentation in Galatians 1:1 is the starting point not of a defensive but an offensive sort of argument. He first strengthened his position as an envoy of God before he launched his attack on the opponents" (Johan S. Vos, "Paul's Argumentation in Galatians 1-2," *HTR* 87:1 [1994]: 3-4). Also see David Cook ("the Prescript as Programme in Galatians," *JTS* 43 [1992]: 511-19), who argues that the expansions in the prescript are meant eschatologically to present the thematic thrust of the letter, and thereby the prescript replaces the thanksgiving section with Galatians 1:1 functioning as the letter's introduction.

[12]Hillyer, *1 and 2 Peter, Jude* , 25-26.

[13]See D. Edmond Hiebert, "Designation of the Readers in 1 Peter 1:1-2," *BSac* 137 (1980): 64-75.

[14]Heinrich Rendtorff, *Getrostes Wandern: Eine Einführung in den ersten Brief des Petrus*, Die urchristliche Botschaft 20 [Hamburg: Furche, 1951], 18. Cf. Bernard Weiss, *Commentary on the New Testament*, vol. 4: *Thessalonians to Revelation*, trans. George Schodde and Epiphanius Wilson [New York, NY: Funk & Wagnalls Co., 1906], 262-64.

also identified the prescript as outlining the metaphorical focus of the letter[15] -- though in regard to the diaspora as the controlling metaphor.[16] Martin further notes that ἐκλεκτοῖς (elect), παρεπιδήμοις (visitors) and διασπορᾶς (diaspora) indicate the three metaphor clusters that structure the letter-body.[17] The diaspora metaphor of 1 Peter is clearly stated at the very outset of the epistle, as it serves as the thrust of the consolatory purpose of the letter.[18] Martin's thesis can be traced back to Goppelt's initial work on the prescript. Goppelt not only understands διασπορᾶς as a Petrine distinction from the Pauline corpus, but he also understands the "diaspora" as central to understanding the Petrine recipients' self-understanding as "a people living in small communal organizations scattered among the peoples and waiting expectantly for its ingathering in the eschaton."[19] In his view, this is a people whose diaspora condition is composed of "ideas about estrangement resulting from election."[20] From this self-perception, the diaspora is explored in the letter programmatically with the above designations.[21]

In reference to the designation ἐκλεκτοῖς παρεπιδήμοις διασπορᾶς, Michaels notes: "The identity of the recipients is a more central concern to the author than his own identity." The terms ἐκλεκτοί and παρεπίδημοι:

---

[15]Martin, *Metaphor and Composition in 1 Peter*, 147.

[16]The metaphorical, rather than literal, nature of διασπορᾶς in 1:1 was also identified by G. W. Blenkin (*The First Epistle General of Peter*, Cambridge Greek Testament for Schools and Colleges [Cambridge: Cambridge University Press, 1914], 10).

[17]Martin, *Metaphor and Composition in 1 Peter*, 160-61.

[18]First Peter is not only a paraenetic letter, but also functions as a consolatory address. The consolatory nature of 1 Peter has been observed and studied by Frederick W. Danker, "1 Peter 1.24-2.17 -- A Consolatory Pericope," *ZNW* 58 (1967): 93-103.

[19]Goppelt, *A Commentary on 1 Peter*, 66.

[20]Goppelt, *A Commentary on 1 Peter*, 66 (full discussion, 64-72).

[21]Cf. James Moffatt (*The General Epistles: James, Peter, and Judas*, The Moffatt New Testament Commentary [London: Hodder and Stoughton, 1947], 89-90), who recognizes the diaspora of 1:1 as both eschatological and programmatical for the other parts of the letter (specifically 2:11).

together sum up the recipients' identity. These terms, nowhere else found in combination in biblical literature, appear on first impression to point in quite different directions. One expresses a relationship to God, the other a relationship to human society. One denotes a privileged group (before God), the other a disadvantaged group (in society). Yet the two expressions do not limit or qualify each other. The addressees are "strangers" because of (not despite) being chosen. Their divine election is a sociological as well as theological fact, for it has sundered them from their social world and made them like strangers or temporary residents in their respective cities and provinces. This is Peter's assumption and the basis on which he writes to them.[22]

The genitive διασπορᾶς, according to Michaels, "further characterizes this community's experience as parallel to that of Israel."[23] According to Michaels, the "diaspora" referred to is not the Jewish diaspora. Rather, the author of 1 Peter

> envisioned a parallel situation among Christians. . . . [H]is readers [did not] belong to the Jewish diaspora or were living as strangers among the dispersed Jews, but ... themselves constituted a diaspora, the only diaspora, in fact, that Peter gives evidence of knowing. He sees them not in relation to the Jews (not even as displacing the Jews in the plan of God) but (like the Jewish diaspora itself) always in relation to 'the Gentiles' (cf. 2:12; 4:3).[24]

Given the importance to the diaspora theme in the prescript, it is noteworthy that Michaels' primary criticism of Troy Martin's *Metaphor and Composition in 1 Peter* is in direct reference it. Michaels states:

---

[22]Michaels, *1 Peter*, 6.

[23]Michaels, *1 Peter*, 10. The socioreligious dynamics of the Jewish diaspora, however, are significant for understanding the Petrine community's self-designation as "diaspora." For a solid overview of the diaspora concept (historical, sociological, and religious aspects within the development of Judaism), see the article by Theodore Reinarch, "Diaspora" (*The Jewish Encyclopedia*, vol. 4: *Chazars-Dreyfus* [New York, NY: KTAV Publishing House, 1906], 559-73); and A. Causse, *Les Dispersés D'Israël: Les origines de la diaspora et son rôle dans la formation du Judaïsme*, Études D'Histoire et de Philosophie Religieuses Publiées par la Faculté de Théologie Protestante de l'Université de Strasburg 19 [Paris: Librarire Félix Alcan, 1929]).

[24]Michaels, *1 Peter*, 8. Also note Beare's (*The First Epistle of Peter*, 75) comments on παρεπιδήμοις that "he whose eyes are fixed upon the eternal can never feel himself anything but a sojourner among things temporal (Cf. Heb. 11:13-16). It is in this sense that the writer imagines the Church as a new Diaspora."

As for the metaphor of the Jewish diaspora, it is indeed significant in 1 Peter, but Martin burdens it with more weight than it can carry. . . . Martin labors to bring all these [metaphor clusters] under the grand umbrella of the diaspora metaphor, but with mixed success. What he demonstrates instead is that no one metaphor so dominates the others that it can explain the structure and the varied rhetorical strategies of this unique letter.[25]

Given Michaels' contention that 1:1-2 function "to identify the recipients of the letter as God's chosen people living as strangers in the diaspora and to lay a theological basis for their identity,"[26] one would expect his support of the diaspora metaphor in 1 Peter, with the prescript bringing this out as part of the "identity of the recipient" and the "theological basis" for the letter.[27] As William G. Doty has observed, "description of the addressees extends to mention of their special status as recipients of the gospel, as holy ones/saints, or as church groups in a particular region."[28] For 1 Peter, the addressees are referred to as constituting a "diaspora." This explains the ontological status of the Petrine community.[29]

---

[25]Michaels, review of Martin's *Metaphor and Composition in 1 Peter*, *JBL* 112 (1993): 359.

[26]Michaels, *1 Peter*, 13.

[27]Similarly, Michaels has also stated a positive case for the diaspora metaphor functioning as the key to the genre of 1 Peter. See his "Jewish and Christian Apocalyptic Letters: 1 Peter, Revelation, and 2 Baruch 78-87" (SBLSP 26, ed. Kent Harold Richards [Atlanta, GA.: Scholars Press, 1987], 268-75; esp. pp. 269-72). The diaspora inclusio of "diaspora" (1:1) and "Babylon" (5:13), as Michaels intriguingly observes, further designate the relational connection between the author and the community (269): "There is a correspondence between 'Babylon' at the end of the letter and 'diaspora' at the beginning: the author and his readers are in the same boat. Instead of a letter from 'home base' [i.e., Jerusalem] to a group of homeless exiles, 1 Peter is a letter from the homeless to the homeless!" Consequently, based upon Michaels' own writings, the diaspora theme/metaphor in 1 Peter does indeed function programmatically and rhetorically for 1 Peter, thereby validating Martin's compositional theory.

[28]William G. Doty, *Letters in Primitive Christianity*, Guides to Biblical Scholarship: New Testament Series (Philadelphia, PA: Fortress Press, 1973), 29.

[29]Claude Lepelley ("Le contexte historique de la Première Lettre de Pierre," in ed. Charles Perrot, *Étude sur la Première Lettre de Pierre*, LD 102 [Paris: Cerf, 1980], 46) also recognizes "diaspora" as a significant indicator of the condition of the Petrine audience, which for Lepelley is primarily related to a persecution theme.

THE TRANSITION FROM THE PRESCRIPT TO THE BLESSING (1:2-3)

The prescript rises to a concluding climax in verse 2 with the dual presentation of "grace" and "peace." Hillyer recognizes the Jewish connotations with this dual greeting in early Christian letters:

> The form of greeting, **grace and peace** (*charis kai eirēnē*), is frequent in NT letters. It is often said that it brings together for the first time the usual Greek greeting, **grace** (*charis*) and the Hebrew greeting **peace** (*sălōm*) -- even if the two terms are not mentioned in what we might regard as "chronological" order. But the likelihood is that the phrase **grace and peace** echoes early Christian worship and derives from the daily Jewish liturgy in the temple, with its priestly blessing of Numbers 6:25-26, "The Lord . . . be *gracious* to you; . . . and give you *peace*."[30]

Although Hillyer's reiteration of the liturgical compositional theory is questionable, he is correct in recognizing the Jewish element of this passage.[31] The fact that the section concludes with a possible allusion to the Hebrew Bible (i.e., Num 6:25-26) is significant.[32] Yet this allusion should not be

---

[30]Hillyer, *1 and 2 Peter, Jude*, 27. Similarly, Davids (*The First Epistle of Peter*, 49-50) states: "To these covenant people Peter extends the typically Pauline greeting 'grace and peace' (used in all Pauline correspondence and not attested to before Paul). This expression is formed from the Greek term 'greeting' (in Greek *chairein*, sounding like the word for grace, *charis*; cf. Jas. 1:1), which was standard in Greek letters but in Paul has been Christianized as a prayer for 'grace,' and the normal Jewish greeting *shalom* or 'peace' (as in Dan. 4:1, 'peace be multiplied'), which was also a wish or prayer for God's blessing of wholeness and prosperity. While this may be the root of the expression, however, one should not put too much weight on it, for its frequent use by Paul means that it had probably become a standard Christian greeting, at least in Pauline circles, by the time 1 Peter was written."

[31]Doty (*Letters in Primitive Christianity*, 29) also recognizes that in the Pauline letters there is a mixture of Greek and Jewish influence, such as in this "grace and peace" formulaic expression.

[32]Due to the reference to "peace . . . in abundance," the allusion to peace may also be derived from Daniel 4:1; 6:25 LXX. Hillyer notes that the ordering of "grace and peace" can also be found in 2 Maccabees 1:1-2 (*1 and 2 Peter, Jude*, 30). Cf. F. J. A. Hort (*The First Epistle of St. Peter: I.1-- II.17* [London: Macmillan and Co., Limited, 1898], 25), who also understands Numbers 6:25-26 (the "Aaronic Benediction") as the probable source for this formulaic expression; see also J. W. C. Wand, *The General Epistles of St. Peter and St. Jude*, Westminster Commentaries (London: Methuen & Co. Ltd., 1934), 40.

overemphasized.[33]   According   to   Fitzmyer,   Aramaic   letters
followed either a "peace" greeting formula or the more personal "well wish"
greeting formula.[34] Furthermore, Jewish parallels exist where χάρις and εἰρήνη
appear in combination.[35] The "grace and peace" formula can be found throughout
early Christian letters, most notably the Pauline collection. As L. G. Champion
articulated, the "grace and peace" formula found in the Pauline letters more likely
relates to early Christian worship language.[36] The worship context, which is
adapted for the epistolary medium of communication, is broader than the Pauline
mission, and, therefore, reflects early Christian circles in a very broad and general
sense.[37] Consequently, a direct or conscious reliance upon the Jewish scriptures
in verse 2 may not be the case.[38]

The use of the formula may be significant. According to Hillyer, this
formula defines "in a nutshell the extent of the mighty benefits of Christ's saving

---

[33]Davids (*The First Epistle of Peter*, 50) correctly cautions definitively correlating the
Jewish/Greek source for this formulaic expression. Robert Johnston (*First Epistle of Peter: Revised
Text with Introduction and Commentary* [Edinburgh: T. & T. Clark, 1888 (reprinted: Minneapolis, MN:
James Family Publishing Company, 1978)], 51-52) also finds the Jewish/Greek correlation of εἰρήνη
and χάρις questionable.

[34]Fitzmyer, "Some Notes on Aramaic Epistolography," 214-15.

[35]Kazuhito Shimada ("Formulary Material in First Peter: A Study According to the Method of
Traditionsgeschichte" [Th.D. diss., Union Theological Seminary, 1966], 128-29) refers to "the Salutatio
of the petition for authorization to rebuild the Temple of Yaho (dated 407 B.C.) as found among the
Elphantine papyri" as well as *1 Enoch* 5:7 and (with "mercy" instead of "grace") the *Syriac Apocalypse
of Baruch* 78:2.

[36]L. G. Champion, *Benedictions and Doxologies in the Epistles of Paul* (Oxford: Kemp Hall Press,
1934), 29: "It is often held that this sentence arose through a combination of the Jewish greeting
εἰρήνη ὑμῖν, with the greeting χαίρειν customary in Greek letters, which by the Christians was
changed to χάρις. But the facts given above lend weight to the suggestion of E. Lohmeyer that the
whole phrase was first formulated in the Christian worship and then taken over by Paul into his letters."

[37]Champion, *Benedictions and Doxologies*, 31-32. Also see Shimada's ("Formulary Material,"
107-38) discussion of the Petrine prescript, especially in relation to Pauline influence on the
development of the salutation formula "grace and peace."

[38]See also W. H. Bennett (*The General Epistles: James, Peter, John, and Jude*, The Century Bible
[Edinburgh: T.C. & E.C. Jack, 1901], 187-88) for non-Jewish/Christian Egyptian parallels.

acts."[39]   These benefits are relational in essence: grace being the basis for the believer's relationship with God and peace "the soul's inward rich enjoyment of that divine bounty."[40]   Thus, the prescript ends with a Jewish/Christian formula that typified the positive aspects of their diaspora condition: their allegiance with God.[41]

The conclusion of the prescript of 1 Peter and the beginning of the blessing-section are nicely balanced. By concluding with a high note of the positive reception of God's grace and peace, the author shifts to a section of praise:

> Εὐλογητὸς ὁ θεὸς καὶ πατὴρ τοῦ κυρίου ἡμῶν ᾽Ιησοῦ Χριστοῦ, ὁ κατὰ τὸ πολύ αὐτοῦ ἔλεος ἀναγεννήσας ἡμᾶς εἰς ἐλπίδα ζῶσαν δι᾽ ἀναστάσεως ᾽Ιησοῦ Χριστοῦ ἐκ νεκρῶν...

> Blessed be the God and Father of our Lord Jesus Christ; by his abundant mercy he has given us new birth into a living hope through the resurrection of Jesus Christ from the dead... (NRSV slightly modified).

This transition from the focus on the community to the focus on God is accomplished with the opening "Blessed be" in verse 3. The correlation between the community's reception of grace and peace and the praise to God is clearly

---

[39]Hillyer, *1 and 2 Peter, Jude*, 27.

[40]Hillyer, *1 and 2 Peter, Jude*, 27. Similarly, see Beare, *The First Epistle of Peter*, 77. J. N. D. Kelly (*A Commentary on the Epistles of Peter and of Jude*, Black's New Testament Commentaries [London: A. and C. Black, 1969], 45) understands "peace" in verse 2 as Jewish in connotation. Kelly argues that "the OT 'peace' (Heb. *shālōm*) was much richer in content than the Greek (*eirēnē*) or Latin (*pax*) equivalents, including all blessings, material and spiritual, bestowed on man by God, more particularly in the eschatology of the prophets . . . the salvation which He will bring in about in the Messianic age. . . . it is the objective condition of being right with God, with all the blessedness which flows from that."

[41]Cranfield (*The First Epistle of Peter*, 18-19) recognizes an eschatological meaning behind this formula. His statement that "peace of the Messiah, peace as equivalent of salvation" takes precedence over "the other meanings, reconciliation between man and God, between man and man, and peace as peace of mind" (19) is putting to narrow a parameter around "eschatological" peace. Instead, it would be best to see "reconciliation" peace, such as here in 1:2, being an expression of God's eschatological-soteriological activity (see also his, *I & II Peter and Jude*, Torch Bible Commentaries [London: SCM Press Ltd., 1960], 33).

established with the reference to "new birth" and "a living hope," both of which relate back to the grace and peace of verse 2. Hillyer observes that, "the experiences of *new birth* and of a *living hope* are beyond human procurement. They are God's gracious gift and are bestowed solely on account of *his great mercy*."[42] It is because this new birth/living hope condition is only considered to derive from God's grace that God is worthy of the praise given in the blessing-section.[43] From the consolatory concern of the author for the community, the transition to the blessing-section from the prescript-section continues and heightens the positive aspects of the community situation. The author correlates the community's well-being with their relational standing with God.[44]

Contrary to Hillyer's position, Michaels contends that the terms χάρις and εἰρήνη do not designate any significance in anticipating themes within 1 Peter, due to merely being part of a normal early Christian letter (e.g., Pauline epistles; Revelation; 2 Peter; 2 John; *1 Clement*; and with "mercy" replacing "grace" in Jude; Polycarp's *Letter to the Philippians*; and *The Martyrdom of Polycarp*).[45] Michaels' contention, although valid, must be scrutinized according to the literary

---

[42]Hillyer, *1 and 2 Peter, Jude*, 31. Similarly, Hort understands 1:3-12 as preparing "the way for exhortations and instruction by drawing the converts upward toward the height of the 'grace' into which they have been received" (*The First Epistle of St. Peter*, 27). I have translated πολύ as "abundant" rather than "great" in order to indicate the sense of fullness, rather than magnitude, that is being presented in this verse. The idea of "abundant mercy" in verse 3, furthermore, reflects back to πληθυνθείη ("multiplied" or "abundant") in verse 2. This further indicates the rhetorical interconnection between verses 2 and 3.

[43]Hort (*The First Epistle of St. Peter*, 26) recognizes that "the word *grace*, standing at the head of the Christian form of blessing, directs our thoughts to the heavenly source of blessing." Hort does not, however, see any significant meaning lying behind εἰρήνη, holding instead that it refers to a lack of conflict. "Peace" is interpreted as subordinate to "grace."

[44]Dijkman ("The Socio-Religious Condition of the Recipients of 1 Peter: An Attempt to Solve the Problems of Date, Authorship and Addressees of the Letter" [Ph.D. diss., University of Witwatersrand (Johannesburg, South Africa)], 39) indicates that the hope of the blessing is not only interested in the present dilemma faced by the Petrine community, but is also eschatological in orientation. Dijkman understands this as the Petrine presentation of the parousia "as the fulfillment of the Old Testament hope."

[45]See Michaels, *1 Peter*, 13.

context within which the formula is utilized. Did the author of 1 Peter merely follow early Christian convention, or did he use a typical formula for a specific reason? Only the contextual usage of the formula can determine the correct answer to this question.

The end of the prescript does indeed indicate a significant break in the text. The usage of the early Christian formula χάρις ὑμῖν καὶ εἰρήνη (v. 2b) typically functioned to conclude the prescript-section of an early Christian letter.[46] In 1 Peter, as Schutter has correctly observed,[47] this formula in 1:2b is paralleled with 5:14, where a "peace" wish is passed along to the recipients to conclude the letter. Schutter's inclusio concept, however, does not rely so much on the closing "grace and peace" formula in 1:2, but rather is designated in 1:1/5:13 with ἐκλεκτοῖς/συνεκλεκτή. Schutter identifies four compositional devices in this regard: (1) "it is subtly reinforced by the designation of the recipients in the opening as παρεπιδήμοις διασπορᾶς and of the sending community in the closing as resident ἐν Βαβυλῶνι"; (2) the foreshadowing of "ideas predominant within the letter" such as "alien status (1.17, 2.11), election (2.4ff.), foreknowledge (1.4f., 12, 20), God as Father (1.3, 17), holiness (1.15f., 2.5ff., 3.5), obedience (1.14, 22), and the blood of Jesus (1.19)"; (3) in the closing "the retrospective motivation-for-writing formula itself that summarizes the letter's contents"; and (4) also in the closing, "the benediction that echoes the key-word, 'peace,' which is first sounded in the opening salutation."[48] Thus, the peace formula is only one contributing factor to the compositional inclusio of the whole letter, which is

---

[46]Πληθυνθείη ("multiplied") is an expansion upon the typical "grace and peace" formula, and may be part of a variant formulaic expression of "grace and peace." Hort (*The First Epistle of St. Peter*, 26), William Kelly (*The First Epistle of Peter* [London: T. Weston, 1904], 14), Best (*1 Peter*, 73) and George Benson (*A Paraphrase of the Seven (Commonly Called) Catholic Epistles* [London: J. Waugh, 1749], 168) claim Daniel 3:98 (LXX) as the source for this expansion -- an expansion also used in Jude, 2 Peter, *1 Clement*, *Epistle to Polycarp*, *Martyrdom of Polycarp*, and *Apostolic Constitutions*.

[47]Schutter, *Hermeneutic and Composition in 1 Peter*, 28.

[48]Schutter, *Hermeneutic and Composition in 1 Peter*, 28, ftn. 41.

primarily structured according to the diaspora concept. Significant, though, is the fact that the fourth compositional device is at the transitional point from the prescript to the blessing-section.

What is significant in regard to the transitional motion from verse 2 to verse 3 is the fact that there is a definite break in the text. Εὐλογητὸς ὁ θεὸς καὶ πατὴρ τοῦ κυρίου ἡμῶν Ἰησοῦ Χριστοῦ (v. 3a) is followed by a series of relative clauses running to the end of verse 12.[49] Consequently, verse 3a sets the stage for the blessing-section. This is a typical technique used in 1 Peter, i.e., the author states at the outset of a section, or subsection, the primary theme or thrust of the section, and then develops an exposition on this opening statement.[50]

An important shift occurs from a focus upon the recipients (prescript) to a focus on the divine realm (blessing). The opening of the blessing-section is typical of the opening of early Christian prayers.[51] One such example is P. Oxy. 925 (5th or 6th century):

> Ὁ θ(εὸ)ς ὁ παντοκράτωρ ὁ ἅγιος ὁ ἀληθινὸς φιλάνθρωπος καὶ δημιουργὸς ὁ π(ατ)ὴρ τοῦ κ(υρίο)υ (καὶ) σω(τῆ)ρ(ο)ς ἡμῶν Ἰ(ησο)ῦ Χ(ριστο)ῦ, φανέρωσόν μοι τὴν παρὰ σοὶ ἀλήθιαν εἰ βούλῃ με ἀπελθεῖν εἰς Χιούτ. ἢ εὑρίσκω σε σὺν ἐμοὶ πράττοντα (καὶ) εὐμενήν; γένοιτο, [abbrev. for "amen"].

---

[49]If the ἐν ᾧ of the opening clause in verse 6 is taken as absolute, thereby "in this you now rejoice" or "rejoice in this" (NRSV), then the running sentence could be broken at the end of verse 5 rather than running to the end of verse 12. The antecedent for ἐν ᾧ, however, is clearly ἐν καιρῷ ἐσχάτῳ in verse 5 (see Martin, *Metaphor and Composition in 1 Peter*, 62). Thus, this dependent clause continues the nominal sentence rather than beginning a new sentence.

[50]See, for example, the discussion of 1:13 below and 3:13 (Appendix 3).

[51]Selwyn (*The First Epistle of St. Peter*, 121-22) notes that "the blessing of God was a characteristic feature of Jewish prayer, and became focused in the *Shemoneh 'Esreh* or Eighteen Benedictions, which were recited thrice daily in the Synagogue." J. N. D. Kelly (*A Commentary on the Epistles of Peter and of Jude*, 47) also understands "Blessed be" in reference to Jewish prayers, yet adapted by early Christians christologically (thus, the ". . . of our Lord Jesus Christ" addition). Similarly, see Cranfield (*The First Epistle of Peter*, 20) who recognizes this as a tool for encouraging the Petrine community; and Best, *1 Peter*, 74. For Jewish parallels of a eulogical formula, see Shimada ("Formulary Material," 141-44, 146).

O God almighty, holy, true, benevolent, Creator, Father of our Lord
and Saviour Jesus Christ, reveal to me thy truth, whether it is thy
will that I go to Chiot. Shall I find thee aiding me and gracious?
So be it; Amen.[52]

The word order of both 1 Peter and P. Oxy 925 places the subject (ὁ θεός)
near the opening of the section. In P. Oxy. 925, the subject takes the vocative
case in function, while the nominative is found in 1 Peter. This difference can be
discerned as a difference in genre -- P. Oxy. 925 being a prayer rather than a
paraenetic letter (in this particular passage, 1:3-5 is best seen as a "call to
worship").[53] The subject, in both cases, is "God." There is a sense of exclamation
and praise in the opening clause of both texts. Doty indicates that "Hellenistic
letters often have thanksgiving sections which state that the writer 'gives thanks
to the gods' or that the writer 'makes continual mention of you before the gods,'
followed by the reasons that the gods are being thanked -- usually because the
gods have saved the writer or the addressee from some calamity."[54] The
functional purpose of the blessing-section in 1 Peter can be understood along the
lines of this thanksgiving motif, though packaged as a "blessing" rather than
"thanksgiving" in form. The purpose of 1 Peter 1:3 is to shift the focus from the
grace given, the soteriological act, to the source of that grace, God as the rescuer
of the Petrine community.[55] In P. Oxy. 925, this emphatic praise is accomplished

---

[52]*Select Papyri*, LCL 1:440-41.

[53]The Petrine blessing-section is an important expansion on the typical prayer formula in ancient
letters, that followed the health wish. Normally, as in the papyri letters studied by White (*The Form
and Function of the Body of the Greek Letter: A Study in the Letter-Body in the Non-Literary Papyri
and in Paul the Apostle*, SBLDS 2 [Missoula, MT: University of Montana], 1972), the prayer formula
constituted the closing element in the salutation. In 1 Peter (as in many early Christian letters) the
prayer formula has been expanded into its own independent section. Bennett (*The General Epistles*,
188) believes that this opening formula emerged from early Christian worship.

[54]Doty, *Letters in Primitive Christianity*, 31.

[55]Despite White's observations on the Pauline adaptions to the thanksgiving-section of ancient
letters, 1 Peter does indeed follow the basic concepts of the Hellenistic thanksgiving statement. White
states that the Pauline occasion for the thanksgiving is no longer the salvation from the Gods from a
calamity, but rather the congregation's faithfulness to God. In 1 Peter, however, the blessing functions

by the string of titles following the subject proper. These titles stand in apposition to the vocative, thereby modifying θεός with titles of glory.[56]

The presence of εὐλογητός in 1 Peter 1:3 adds an equivalent praiseful emphasis for the Petrine blessing-section.[57] Shimada distinguishes this eulogical formula from doxology and aretalogy formulae. He defines a "eulogical formula" as "a formula of exclamatory prescription of praise to God." Doxology is defined as "a formula which ascribes glory (*doxa*) to God, and often takes the form of 'To Him be glory'." Aretalogy is defined as "a formula of praise of God's (or Christ's) 'wonderful deeds'."[58] In 1 Peter 1:3, however, the distinction is not significant, as all three meanings of this formulaic expression (eulogy, doxology, and aretalogy) suit 1 Peter's epistolary and thematic context well. The further qualification in verse 3, πατὴρ τοῦ κυρίου ἡμῶν Ἰησοῦ Χριστοῦ, is a titular formula that is not uncommon in early Christian literature.[59] Here this genitive qualification adds further emphasis on the greatness for God. Similarly, P. Oxy 925 also contains a variant of this titulary formula, adding σωτῆρος ἡμῶν, "our saviour," to the formula. Consequently, the opening of the blessing-section is similar to the

---

to draw the readers' attention to the soteriological and eschatological act of grace that God has supplied. White, "The Structural Analysis of Philemon: A Point of Departure in the Formal Analysis of the Pauline Letter" (paper for the Society of Biblical Literature Seminar on the Form and Function of the Pauline Letters, 1971; Cited in Doty, *Letters in Primitive Christianity*, 23).

[56]See Herbert W. Smyth, *Greek Grammar* (Cambridge, MA: Harvard University Press, 1956), § 1287.

[57]Donald G. Miller ("Deliverance and Destiny: Salvation in First Peter," *Int* 9 [1955]: 413-25) religiously and poetically states: "'Blessed be the God and Father of our Lord Jesus' (1:3) is the outburst of song with which Peter introduces his discussion of salvation" (415-16). This salvation is connected to "the divine initiative" which "is rooted in the divine compassion and unbelievable pity of the Almighty" (416).

[58]Shimada, "Formulary Material," 141, 158.

[59]Cf. Champion, *Benedictions and Doxologies*, 30. Moffatt (*The General Epistles*, 93) interprets this qualification as a Christianization of a Jewish "devout phrase."

opening of this early Christian prayer.[60] Both emphatically emphasize the significance of God, and each subsequently draws the recipients' attention to God.[61]

Similar to an *exordium* or *prooemium*, the Petrine blessing is meant to prepare the audience psychologically for the message of the letter. This is accomplished by attaining their attention and making them well disposed to the writer/message, thereby making them open to instruction.[62] Hort has observed that

---

[60]To postulate that the Petrine blessing-section is liturgical in form, would be an incorrect correlation between 1 Peter and P. Oxy. 925. First Peter may indeed utilize hymnic and liturgical material to formulate the blessing, yet this cannot be established beyond mere conjecture and speculative historical reconstructions of early Christian worship (contra Boismard [*Quatre hymnes baptismale*, 15-56], who attempts to reconstruct an early Christian hymn behind 1 Peter 1:3-5, primarily through a comparative analysis between the Petrine passage and Titus 3, Romans 8:14-25 and Galatians 3:23. He gives a reconstruction of the Petrine "hymne baptismale" on p. 26). Furthermore, there needs to be a clear sensitivity to the epistolary nature and function of the components in 1 Peter, such as the blessing-section. This present comparison between 1 Peter and P. Oxy. 925 is not meant to propose either a liturgical *Sitz* for 1 Peter, nor to suggest any literary connection between the two texts. Rather, P. Oxy. 925 does highlight the "prayerful" nature of the Petrine blessing. I. Howard Marshall (*1 Peter*, IVP New Testament Commentary Series [Downers Grove, IL: InterVarsity Press, 1991], 35) recognizes that "Peter starts with an expression of praise that is exactly the same as the wording used in 2 Corinthians 1:3 and Ephesians 1:3. This shows that this form of words had become traditional in the church, probably widely used in prayer and praise in the church meetings." Clark Palmer's ("The Use of Traditional Materials in Hebrews, James, and 1 Peter" [Ph.D. diss., Southwest Baptist Theological Seminary, 1985], 178-79) contention, however, that 1:3-12 is "a liturgical prayer" is unfounded due internal evidence: the nominative in 1:3 clearly signifies that "God" is the subject of the blessing and not the addressee. Rather, the Petrine community addressed in the prescript is the addressee of the blessing. This signifies the "call to worship" nature of the Petrine blessing over against Palmer's liturgical prayer hypothesis. If the blessing were indeed a prayer redacted into the letter, then the vocative would have been utilized as it is in P. Oxy. 925. For the Petrine author, such traditions seem to be drawn upon in formulating the "call to worship" used to open the blessing-section. Selwyn (*The First Epistle of St. Peter*, 122) recognized the Jewish influence upon 1 Peter, when he stated that "the blessing in 1 Pet. i.3ff. is not a hymn but a Christian *Shema.*" Similarly, Davids (*The Epistle of Peter*, 51) perceives a strong Jewish (Biblical) influence on 1:3. See also Shimada, "Formulary Material," 149-53.

[61]Despite his conjectural attempt to reconstruct a baptismal hymn behind this passage, Boismard (*Quatre hymnes baptismale*, 26-27) is correct in stating: "Dès les premiers mots, cette hymne baptismale *plonge le chrétien dans le grand courant d' action* de grâces que le peuple d' Israël ne cessait de faire monter vers Dieu pour le remercier des bienfaits reçus de lui" [emphasis mine].

[62]Johan S. Vos ("Paul's Argumentation," 4-5) has correctly cautioned against broadening the concept of *exordium* to the point where it has lost its functional meaning, which is "the function of making the readers well-disposed, attentive, and ready to receive instruction. As such the function of the *exordium* is preparatory. The accent lies on the psychological aspect: the purpose of the *exordium* is to make the hearts of the readers well disposed" (5). See Quintilian, *Inst.Orat.* 4.1.5 and Aristotle,

θεὸς πατήρ, as a designation, has a definite purpose in New Testament usage.[63] This is true of 1 Peter, as πατήρ indicates the familial relationship of God to Jesus and subsequently to the Petrine community. This paternal theme is noted and developed in the first metaphor cluster of the letter-body. Reicke has correctly indicated the rhetorical function of this opening at verse 3. He states that the author's "objective is to help the hearers to recognize the infinite value of the gift they have received: the gospel and their faith."[64] Thus, a clear shift can be discerned in 1 Peter, from a focus on the grace bestowed upon the community to a focus upon the source of that grace. According to Davids, 1 Peter 1:3 "does not focus on the past, the new birth itself, but on the future, for the goal of regeneration is 'a living hope'; that is, it points to a bright future ahead" -- a concept further developed in 1:4.[65] Goppelt has similarly observed this same function of the blessing's opening:

> The expressions of thankfulness and entreaty that normally follow
> the address and greeting in ancient letters are formulated here as

Rhetoric 3.14. Shimada ("Formulary Material," 158) understands 1 Peter 1:3-4 as an eulogical *proemium* drawn from a liturgical setting of the early church. David W. Kendall ("The Literary and Theological Function of 1 Peter 1:3-12," 103-20) has argued extensively that the prescript functions as the introduction for 1:13-5:11, and therefore all the key themes of the paraenetic body (primarily the concept of "saving grace") can be found in this introductory passage. Methodologically, however, it is important to remember that 1:3-12 is not an *exordium*, but rather is a blessing. The distinction must be drawn on the basis of genre: the *exordium* is part of ancient speech, while the blessing being part of epistolary conventions. To force an epistle into the framework of the speech has been a methodological flaw of much of rhetorical criticism. From the perspective of rhetorical function, however, the *exordium* can serve as an illustration of the rhetorical function of the blessing.

[63]Hort, *The First Epistle of St. Peter*, 21.

[64]Reicke, *The Epistles of James, Peter, and Jude*, AB 37 (Garden City, NY: Doubleday & Co., 1964), 79. Cf. Cranfield, *The First Epistle of Peter*, 21 (see also his, *I & II Peter and Jude*, 35). Specifically, Cranfield recognizes the importance of metaphorical language in 1 Peter, beginning with the letter's opening: "To describe what God has done in Christ is far beyond the reach of human words; but, though the attempt must be beggar language, it must nevertheless be made. So Peter resorts to metaphor. God BEGAT US AGAIN UNTO A LIVING HOPE."

[65]Davids, *The First Epistle of Peter*, 52. See also Johnston, *First Epistle of Peter*, 53-54. Demarest (*Commentary on the Catholic Epistles*, 167) commented on the opening of verse 3 as "a sublime outburst of thanksgiving for the gracious ends God has in view in the regeneration of the chosen."

praise to God, as *eulogia*. The eulogy is an OT and Jewish form of prayer. 1 Peter appropriates this precedent by way of Christian tradition.[66]

The use of εὐλογητός in this emphatic sense further signifies the sharp compositional break between the prescript and the blessing-section.

From a rhetorical perspective, the blessing can be seen as epideictic. The Petrine blessing, especially 1:3-5, fits well the definition of epideictic species given by Kennedy: "it is epideictic when he [the rhetor] seeks to persuade them to hold or reaffirm some point of view in the present, as when he celebrates or denounces some person or some quality. Praise or blame is taken by Aristotle to be the characteristic feature of epideictic."[67] Such an epideictic style is not uncommon in proems or epilogues, and, therefore, should not be seen as unusual here in 1 Peter's blessing.[68] The goal of epideictic praise in 1 Peter 1:3-5 is "to secure a favorable hearing" from the recipients.[69] For the Petrine author, this goal is closely related to the soteriological condition of the Petrine community. This relation, along with its rhetorical intent, is evident with the sharp compositional break and the transitional development between 1:2b and 1:3.

---

[66]Goppelt, *A Commentary on 1 Peter*, 78.

[67]Kennedy, *New Testament Interpretation through Rhetorical Criticism*, 19. See Aristotle, *Rhetoric* 1.3.3-7.

[68]Although the ancient rhetorical handbooks strongly emphasized the fact that a document's genus (forensic, deliberative, epideictic) was based upon the audience addressed (see, for example, Aristotle, *Rhetoric* 1.3.3), the epideictic genus served as a "catch all" catagory for what did not fit into forensic or deliberative discourse. Consequently, it is possible to speak of an epideictic flavour, or style, even within another genus. In effect, the deliberative genus of 1 Peter is highlighted with epideictic "extras" here in the letter's opening blessing. The epideictic nature of the blessing serves the Petrine author's rhetorical purposes by setting down the basis upon which the deliberative discourse of the body-middle is to be received.

[69]Kennedy, *New Testament Interpretation through Rhetorical Criticism*, 74.

THE TRANSITION FROM BLESSING TO BODY OPENING (1:10-13)

The conclusion of the blessing-section comprises verses 10-12. This is a climactic point for this section, and contains two significant aspects. The verses read:

Περὶ ἧς σωτηρίας ἐξεζήτησαν καὶ ἐξηραύνησαν προφῆται οἱ περὶ τῆς εἰς ὑμᾶς χάριτος προφητεύσαντες, ἐραυνῶντες εἰς τίνα ἢ ποῖον καιρὸν ἐδήλου τὸ ἐν αὐτοῖς πνεῦμα Χριστοῦ προμαρτυρόμενον τὰ εἰς Χριστὸν παθήματα καὶ τὰς μετὰ ταῦτα δόξας. οἷς ἀπεκαλύφθη ὅτι οὐχ ἑαυτοῖς ὑμιν δὲ διηκόνουν αὐτά, ἃ νῦν ἀνηγγέλη ὑμῖν διὰ τῶν εὐαγγελισαμένων ὑμᾶς [ἐν] πνεύματι ἁγίῳ ἀποσταλέντι ἀπ᾽ οὐρανοῦ, εἰς ἃ ἐπιθυμοῦσιν ἄγγελοι παρακύψαι.

Concerning this salvation, the prophets who prophesied of the grace that was to be yours made careful search and inquiry, inquiring about the person or time that the Spirit of Christ within them indicated when it testified in advance to the sufferings destined for Christ and the subsequent glory. It was revealed to them that they were serving not themselves but you, in regard to the things that have now been announced to you through those who brought you good news by the Holy Spirit sent from heaven -- things into which angels long to look! (NRSV)

First, verses 10-12 are an indirect reference to the Jewish scriptures. Specifically, the author refers to "the prophets" (v. 10). No specific prophet or age of prophets is specified. Rather, the implication is that all the prophetic work of the Jewish scriptures was intended as a testimony "in advance to the sufferings destined for Christ and the subsequent glory" (v. 11). It has been observed that 1 Peter typically draws upon the Jewish scriptures to emphasize Petrine christology, which is closely connected to Petrine eschatology. This is accomplished by adapting the particular passage for the present context.[70]

---

[70]See Jacques Schlosser, "Ancien Testament et Christologie dans la *Prima Petri*," in ed. Charles Perrot, *Étude sur la Première Lettre de Pierre*, LD 102 (Paris: Cerf, 1980), 70-72, 93-96.

Therefore, there is a clear reference to the Jewish scriptures, albeit not a direct quotation, allusion, or midrash.

E. G. Selwyn, contrary to the scriptural understanding of προφῆται, has advanced the theory that προφῆται refers to Christian prophets. This position is postulated due to the absence of the definite article in 1 Peter 1:10, contrary to Matthew 5:17; 7:12 and Luke 16:16 where the article appears.[71] Selwyn's argument has been effectively refuted by Best, Michaels, Martin, and Davids,[72] and, therefore, need not detain us further. A scriptural allusion is surely the best reading of 1:10-12.

Second, the closing of the blessing-section has an eschatological climax. This climax is the age of Christ -- toward which all previous ages moved and for which they were preparatory (v. 12a). As Jean Calloud aptly states: "Le récit est rétrospectif. La bénédiction est surtout prospective."[73] Calloud's statement summarizes well the thematic thrust of not only the transition from the prescript into the blessing, but also for the blessing-section as a whole. There is, in essence, a sense of forward movement. Beare has identified the rhetorical presence of paronomasia in 1 Peter 1:10, "made earnest quest and query," a phrase taken from 1 Maccabees 9:26. Thus, a sense of rhetorical "earnestness" begins

---

[71]Selwyn, *The First Epistle of Peter*, 259-68.

[72]Best, *1 Peter*, 83-84, Michaels, *1 Peter*, 40-41, Martin *Metaphor and Composition in 1 Peter*, 154, Davids, *The First Epistle of Peter*, 60-61. Revere F. Weidner (*Annotations on the General Epistles of James, Peter, John, and Jude and the Revelation of St. John* [New York, NY: Charles Scribners Sons, 1905], 111) asserts that the presence of προφῆται "without the article in Greek, [denotes] prophets as a class." Selwyn's proposal, furthermore, has gained little acceptance, as is evident by Goppelt holding to the traditional Jewish prophetical perspective, within a parallel discussion with the Qumran texts (*A Commentary on 1 Peter*, 96-101). Also note Johnston's (*First Epistle of Peter*, 76-77) refutation of Selwyn's position (which was presented by E. H. Plumptre [*The General Epistles of St. Peter & St. Jude*, The Cambridge Bible for Schools (Cambridge: Cambridge University Press, 1879), 97-98] in the previous century). Also see Monnier, *La Première Épître de l' Apôtre Pierre* (Macon: Protat Frères, 1900), 48; and W. Kelly, *First Epistle of Peter*, 43. Recently, Schutter (*Hermeneutic and Composition in 1 Peter*, 102-3) has taken a neutral stance in identifying the "prophets," preferring, rather, to outline the implications of both meanings in his exegetical work.

[73]Jean Calloud, "Ce que parler veut dire (1 P 1,10-12)," in *Étude sur la Première Lettre de Pierre*, ed. Charles Perrot, LD 102 (Paris: Cerf, 1980), 176.

this climax.[74] Of interest, however, is the glorious finale of the blessing: "into which angels long to look!"[75] Pearson has noted the role of paronomasia throughout 1:3-12, with paronomasia present in the climactic finale (v. 12) as follows:

> to whom it was revealed
> > that not to themselves but to you
> > > they ministered the same things which now were
> > > announced [ἀνηγγέλη] to you [through those
> > > who brought you the good news;
> > > διὰ τῶν εὐαγγελισαμένων]
> > > by the Holy Spirit sent from heaven
> into which things (heaven's) announcers [ἄγγελοι] long to look.[76]

The presence of paronomasia in 1 Peter 1:12, as outlined here, places an emphasis upon the proclamation theme of this eschatological climax. This emphasis, consequently, adds a sense of forward movement within the soteriological-eschatological drama of this text.

The summation of the gospel is a highly positive portrayal of the condition of the community. Johnston observes that the plural δόξας christologically entails the process, or stages, by which Christ attained his "glories," i.e. "the various *stages* of our Lord's course of triumph, the Resurrection, Ascension,

---

[74]Beare, *The First Epistle of Peter*, 90-91. Beare states that 1 Peter 1:10 and its source, 1 Maccabees 9:26, both "give emphatic expression to the earnestness with which enlightenment was sought. Cf. Socrates' description of his lifelong search into the meaning of the oracle which pronounced him the wisest of men (*Apol.* 23A) -- ζητῶ καὶ ἐρευνῶ καὶ τὸν θεόν" (90). Cf. also the *Gospel of Thomas*, where the "searching" theme plays a significant role, particularly in the opening where life and searching for meaning to the words of Jesus are closely related (*Gos. Thom.* 1).

[75]See Charles Bigg, *A Critical and Exegetical Commentary on the Epistles of St. Peter and St. Jude*, The International Critical Commentary, 2nd ed. (Edinburgh: T. & T. Clark, 1902), 111-12. A novel suggestion has been made by Robert L. Webb ("The Apocalyptic Perspective of First Peter" [Th.M. Thesis, Regent College, Vancouver, B.C., 1986], 220-222), who presents the hypothesis that the verbs ἐπιθυμέω and παρακύπτω in 1:12b may indicate an unfulfilled desire of the angels to "know the precise 'time and circumstances' of the eschatological salvation" (222).

[76]Pearson, "The Christological Hymnic Pattern of 1 Peter," 113. The translation is Pearson's, which is based upon the NRSV and her reading of the Greek text. I have, in editorial brackets, adjusted the translation slightly and added the key Greek terms.

Mediatorial Reign, and Second Coming."[77] Davids has correctly recognized the psychological impact that this finale would have had on the Petrine community, when he states that

> the sense of privilege that the readers should have actually [been] living in the time of fulfillment that the prophets longed to experience is underlined by mentioning "which things angels desire to look into". . . . Although suffering, these believers are a privileged people.[78]

This climax reflects back to the opening of the blessing-section (v. 3) and the conclusion of the prescript (v. 2). As Cranfield has accurately described this concluding section of the blessing, "the last three verses of this section are concerned with the praises of salvation."[79] Consequently, a epideictic tone of praise can be discerned running throughout the entire blessing-section.

Significant is the fact that this eschatological climax functions as an emphatic concluding thrust in preparation for the next section.[80] Paton J. Gloag has recognized both the significance and the uniqueness of Petrine eschatology. For Gloag, the eschatology of 1 Peter is closely tied to the consolatory concerns of the author, and, therefore, interweave suffering and glory together along such a consolatory agenda. Gloag understands that "hope is the centre of all his

---

[77]Johnston, *First Epistle of Peter*, 80. Best (*1 Peter*, 81-82) also understands "glories" in reference to a succession of events. In regard to the antithesis between "sufferings" and "glories," see Jean Monnier, *La Première*, 53-54 and Schutter, *Hermeneutic and Composition in 1 Peter*, 123.

[78]Davids, *The First Epistle of Peter*, 64-65. See also Demarest, *Commentary on the Catholic Epistles*, 176; and Best, *1 Peter*, 83.

[79]Cranfield, *The First Epistle of Peter*, 28 (see also his, *1 & II Peter and Jude*, 43).

[80]This is a very positive portrayal, so as to offer comfort and joy to the readers. See John Rogers, *A Godly & Fruitful Exposition Upon all the First Epistle of Peter* [London: Printed by John Field, 1650], 55.

[1 Peter's] exhortations."[81] This implies, in application to our present passage, that the hope of 1:13 is the successive theme from the eschatological climax of 1:10-12,[82] and, thereby, "hope" sets the stage for the paraenetical exhortations following the eschatological theme of hope.[83]

The body-opening (1:13) functions as a complete transitional section of the letter. As Martin observes, it "functions as the transition from the blessing section to the body of the letter."[84] The letter's "principal occasion . . . is usually indicated" in this section.[85] This occasion has been identified as emerging from

---

[81]Paton J. Gloag, *Introduction to the Catholic Epistles* (Edinburgh: T. & T. Clark, 1887), 172-73: "Peter looks forward to a future state of blessedness as the great source of comfort and support to his readers exposed to sufferings and persecution. The night was dark, but it would be followed by a glorious morning. The Epistle is full of joy and consolation. There was a world beyond the grave, where believers would be abundantly recompensed for all the sufferings they now endure for the sake of religion. They were called to an inheritance, incorruptible and undefiled, and that fadeth not away (chap. i. 4). They would receive the end of their faith, even the salvation of their souls (chap. i. 9). When the chief Shepherd shall appear, they would receive the crown of glory that fadeth not away (chap. v. 4). After they had endured temporary sufferings, the God of all graces would make them perfect, and call them to His eternal glory by Christ Jesus (chap. v. 10). Hope is the centre of all his exhortations." Cf. Bennett, *The General Epistles*, 195.

[82]Dijkman ("The Socio-Religious Condition of the Recipients of I Peter," 39) articulates this position: "While this hope may be directed towards God's present deliverance from distress, it is more specifically associated with the eschatological future. In 1 Peter there is a similar emphasis on the parousia when the resurrection of Jesus is interpreted as the fulfillment of the Old Testament hope." Interestingly, Dijkman's comments are in relation to 1 Peter 1:3. Yet these same observations apply equally, if not moreso, to 1:10-12. Thus, the blessing's opening and closing articulate the eschatological thrust of 1 Peter. The rhetorical "climax" may be seen in 1 Peter 1:10-12. Kennedy states: "A less common, but quite effective figure is *climax*, where the thought is emphasized or clarified and given an emotional twist as if by climbing a ladder" (*New Testament Interpretation through Rhetorical Criticism*, 27-28). Kennedy's comment on climax applies to 1:10-12, where a "building-up" to an eschatological thrust occurs. Unlike Romans 5:3-4, where the "ladder" is far clearer, 1 Peter 1:10-12 utilizes salvation history to move the reader up an emphatic "ladder." If this is true, then the emphatic function of the blessing's closing becomes all the more evident.

[83]Note Goppelt's comments on 1:10-11 (*A Commentary on I Peter*, 35): "With the aid of the OT 1 Peter understands the Christian message and the transformation of the human situation through it as eschatological fulfillment event (1:10f)." Also see Moffatt, *General Epistles*, 102.

[84]Martin, *Metaphor and Composition in 1 Peter*, 71. Similarly, Moffatt (*General Epistles*, 104) understands 1:13 as a "bridge" between 1:3-12 and the moral exhortations that begin at 1:14.

[85]White, *The Form and Function of the Body of the Greek Letter*, 33.

the imperative ἐλπίσατε ("hope").[86] The significance of this imperative has led several scholars to see "hope" as the thematic thrust of 1 Peter.[87] J. H. L. Dijkman, furthermore has argued for a Hebraic background for the Petrine concept of hope.[88] Perhaps a better way of perceiving the role of ἐλπίσατε within the overall strategy of 1 Peter is to see the emergence of the consolatory concern of the author and the use of the rhetorical strategy of suppression within this letter. Hope is presented in verse 13 to indicate the concern that the author has for the Petrine community.[89] This concern is in regard to potential defection away from the Christian faith, which would, consequently, result in the recipients' missing out on the eschatological "glory" indicated in the blessing-section (specifically the eschatological climax of verses 10-12). Goppelt has suggested that "with the aid of the OT 1 Peter understands the Christian message and the transformation of the human situation through it as eschatological fulfillment event."[90] This observation

---

[86]Martin, *Metaphor and Composition in 1 Peter*, 71.

[87]Gloag, *Introduction to the Catholic Epistles*, 173-174; Dijkman, "The Socio-Religious Condition of the Recipients of I Peter," 46 (he sees hope as "one of the main threads of thought in this epistle"); Marshall, *1 Peter*; Brox, *Der erste Petrusbrief*, 17; Goppelt, *A Commentary on 1 Peter*, 105-121 (understands 1:13-21 as dominated by the theme of hope); Charles R. Eerdman, *The General Epistles: An Exposition* (Philadelphia, PA: Westminster Press, 1918), 52, 56-57; Samuel McPheeters Glasgow, *The General Epistles: Studies in the Letters of James, Peter, John and Jude*, Brief Book Studies (New York, NY: Fleming H. Revell Company, 1928); William G. Moorehead, *Outline Studies in the New Testament* (Pittsburgh, PA: United Presbyterian Board of Publication, 1910), 40-41; Robertson, "The Use of Old Testament Quotations and Allusions in the First Epistle of Peter." See also Kendall, "1 Peter 1:3-9. On Christian Hope," *Int* 41 (1987): 66-71; and R. P. Martin, *The Theology of the Letters of James, Peter, and Jude*, passim. However, as Floyd V. Filson ("Partakers With Christ: Suffering in First Peter," *Int* 9 [1955]: 410) so aptly put the matter: "There are many scholars who say that First Peter's theme is hope. This seems an exaggeration. The central theme is suffering. And in meeting suffering, as we have seen, the author does much more than point to a future hope."

[88]Dijkman ("The Socio-Religious Condition of the Recipients of I Peter," 39), in his comments on 1 Peter 1:3, states: "The concept of hope in 1 Peter is essentially determined by the Old Testament where it is generally regarded as confidence in God's protection and help. Hence specific objects of hope are less frequently mentioned than the basis of hope, namely, God, His faithfulness, or His name."

[89]Marshall (*1 Peter*, 36): "*Hope* is a key word in the letter and sets the tone for Peter's intense concern with the future of Christians living in a hostile world (see 1:13, 21; 3:5, 15)."

[90]Goppelt, *A Commentary on 1 Peter*, 35.

on 1:10 is correct, for the eschatological climax is the conclusion to the soteriological drama that begins with the prophets. This soteriological-eschatological drama is closely tied to Petrine pneumatology, as Davids has noted.[91] This is the basis for the hope in 1 Peter. The "rhetorical strategy of suppression" is used throughout 1 Peter to accomplish this consolatory goal.[92] Consequently, the negative possibility of defection is not mentioned. Rather, the author has placed an emphasis upon the positive aspects of Christianity. The form that this concern and strategy takes is paraenesis, as Martin has correctly and definitively established.[93] We can observe this in 1:13 with the beginning of the imperatives which run throughout the letter from this point onward.[94]

---

[91]Davids, *The First Epistle of Peter*, 64: ". . . it is announced not because people have discovered the true meaning of Scripture but because the same Spirit who inspired the prophets has been sent from heaven to inspire the messengers, who in turn show the true meaning of the prophets. This fact could be important to Peter for three reasons: (1) the identity of the Spirit guaranteed a correct interpretation, (2) the Spirit was the power behind the message (as in Acts 1:8; 5:32; 1 Cor. 2:4), and (3) the presence of the Spirit among them was the sign that the new age had indeed dawned (as in Acts 2:16-21)." According to Beare (*The First Epistle of Peter*, 54-55), Petrine pneumatology differs from Pauline thought, in that 1 Peter's four references to the Spirit (1:2, 11, 12; 4:14) do not present an indwelling "presence" of the Spirit such as would be expected from Paul. First Peter is seen as having an undeveloped pneumatology (in its preference for a strong theocentric emphasis), which better fits a second generation Christian community than a first generation Christian milieu. Lenski (*Interpretation*, 50) says: "Peter has the climax: prophets-gospel-preachers-angels, all concerned with Christ and our salvation, *the Holy Spirit being back of them all*" (emph. mine). R. P. Martin has emphasized the significance of the Spirit in 1 Peter's theological formulations (*The Theology of the Letters of James, Peter, and Jude*, 117-20).

[92]The phrase "rhetorical strategy of suppression" was coined by Martin, *Metaphor and Composition in 1 Peter*, passim.

[93]Davids (review of Martin, *Metaphor and Composition in 1 Peter*, in *CBQ* 55 [1993]: 594-95) has recognized the significance of Martin's compositional study. Davids states that Martin's study of letter formulas and paraenesis in 1 Peter are definitive (594):

> His data are so extensive and his argument so thorough that I do not believe that these first two conclusions are assailable; they should stand as permanent contributions to the study of 1 Peter.

[94]It has been suggested that ἀγαλλιᾶσθε at 1:6, 8 is an imperative. This imperative reading was postulated by S. F. N. Morus (*Praelectiones in Jacobi et Petri epistolas* [Leipzig: Sumptibus Sommeri, 1794]). Ἀγαλλιᾶσθε can also been understood as an indicative with present meaning (Goppelt, *A Commentary on 1 Peter*; Calvin, *Commentaries on the Catholic Epistles*, 31-35; Beare, *The First Epistle of Peter*, 87, 89 [who recognizes this present "joy" as "the very paradox of Christian faith," (87)]. Another interpretation is to see ἀγαλλιᾶσθε as a present indicative with future

The imperatival force of 1:13 effectively draws the author's discussion away from a focus upon God (the source of grace), and shifts back to a focus upon the community.

Διὸ ἀναζωσάμενοι τὰς ὀσφύας τῆς διανοίας ὑμῶν νήφοντες τελείως ἐλπίσατε ἐπὶ τὴν φερομένην ὑμῖν χάριν ἐν ἀποκαλύψει Ἰησοῦ Χριστοῦ.

Therefore prepare your minds for action; discipline yourselves; set all your hope on the grace that Jesus Christ will bring you when he is revealed.

This compositional transition into the body-opening creates an inclusion around the blessing-section, comprised of the prescript and body-opening. The prescript places the focus upon the Petrine community, which has received "grace and peace." The body-opening emphasizes the community response to the eschatological "grace and peace" they have received.[95] This response is outlined in the imperatival directives given to the community. The blessing-section functions as the source of the grace and peace that the author wishes upon the recipients in verse 2, as well as to be the source for the imperatival directives in verse 13. Consequently, a shift occurs from epideictic to deliberative discourse, with the epideictic blessing serving as the propositional premise for the hortatory

---

meaning (Ps.-Oecumenius, *Commentarii in epistolas catholicas*, 517; also see The Venerable Bede, *Commentary on the Seven Catholic Epistles*, 73; and also Benson, *A Paraphrase*, 175). For Dijkman ("The Socio-Religious Condition of the Recipients of I Peter," 43-44) ἀγαλλιᾶσθε refers to "the joy of the 'End' [which] overflows into the present, lightening the plight of the readers" and thereby reveals that the author of 1 Peter "writes and lives when the expectation of an impending end was still very much alive, namely before 70 AD." Recently, Martin ("The Present Indicative in Petrine Prophetic Statements," paper presented at the Midwest Region of the Society of Biblical Literature, February 19, 1990) has offered a comprehensive study of this issue, and based upon four exegetical issues (mood of ἀγαλλιᾶσθε; time reference of circumstantial participles; gender and antecedent of ᾧ; and the future meaning of a present indicative), determines that ἀγαλλιᾶσθε is best interpreted as a present indicative with future meaning. A summary version of this paper was published by Martin ("The Present Indicative in the Eschatological Statements of 1 Peter 1:6, 8," *JBL* 111 [1992]: 307-14). Therefore, based upon this exegetical discussion, the imperatival statements in 1 Peter should be seen as beginning at 1:13, rather than 1:6.

[95]"Hope" in 1:3 and 1:13 further emphasizes the presence of an inclusio; see Lenski, *Interpretation*, 53.

62

directives of the body-middle.[96] The positive tone of verses 3-12 is significant.
Instead of focusing upon their diaspora condition, of being alienated and
persecuted, the Petrine community is to focus upon the "new birth" (v. 3) and
"inheritance" (v. 4) which they have received "through the resurrection of Jesus
Christ" (v. 3). Therefore, a consolatory emphasis is discernable within the
opening sections of the letter.

The transition from 1:12 to 1:13 closely connects the two sections. The
usage of διό creates a non-definite break, where the body-opening stands in
direct relation to the blessing-section and, thereby, develops directly from the
blessing.[97] In essence, the two compositional units naturally flow into each other.
The usage of διό accomplishes this smooth transitional movement. Lenski
correctly identifies the functional purpose of διό in verse 13, when he states:

> With διό Peter bases his exhortations on the entire preceding
> doxology in which he expects his readers to join. Realizing all that
> this doxology says of them in their blessed relation to God, the
> readers will be ready to respond to the admonitions that are then
> justified.[98]

---

[96]Thurén (*The Rhetorical Strategy of 1 Peter*, 93-98) incorrectly identifies the whole of 1 Peter
as epideictic. Although correct in stating that a forensic genus does not fit 1 Peter (94), he has
misunderstood the nature of epideictic and deliberative discourse. Indeed, Thurén's treatment of the
so-called epideictic elements in 1 Peter, along a shame/honour system, better describes the deliberative
genus. It is best to see 1 Peter as a paraenetic letter and, thus, a deliberative discourse given in
epistolary form. The epideictic nature of the blessing, which fits nicely into epistolary conventions for
blessings or thanksgivings, merely serves as a positive introduction for the letter-body (which is
deliberative). Rhetorically, the blessing functions to set a positive tone (and, subsequently, a premise
for a positive response by the recepients) for the paraenetic thrust of 1 Peter. Thus, 1 Peter is not
epideictic -- it is deliberative with a praiseful introduction that could be called epideictic in flavour.

[97]Selwyn (*The First Epistle of St. Peter*, 139) clearly identifies διό as a transitional device: "the
usual particle when an author passes from statement to inference." This transitional movement has also
been observed by Davids (*1 Peter*, 65), and Bennett (*The General Epistles*, 195, who sees 1:13 being
the practical orientation of "the Christian salvation, as set forth in the previous section"). The same
position is taken by Cranfield (*The First Epistle of Peter*, 31; also, *I & II Peter and Jude*, 46).
Similiarly, see Biggs, *A Critical and Exegetical Commentary on the Epistles of St. Peter and St. Jude*,
112.

[98]Lenski, *Interpretation*, 51. As Martin notes (*Metaphor and Composition in 1 Peter*, 29), Lenski
"is supported by Boismard, Schneider, Spicq, Kelly, Best, Michl, Dendall, and Kistemaker" in this
reading. Also, Hort (*The First Epistle of St. Peter*, 64) and Johnston (*First Epistle of Peter*, 85) take
the same position. Further note Eerdman's comments (*The General Epistles*, 59): "Having given

Therefore, the usage of the transition from 1:12 to 1:13 is one in which the new section develops from the previous one, and the διό conjunction indicates the developmental nature of the body-opening and the blessing-section.

It has been suggested that the opening phrase in 1:13a alludes to Exodus 12:11 ("This is how you shall eat it; your loins girded, your sandals on your feet, and your staff in your hand; and you shall eat it hurriedly. It is the passover of the Lord"). This position has been articulated recently by Hillyer, who perceives verses 12-21 as derivative of "exodus symbolism," and Davids, who sees this possible allusion in connection to 1 Peter's "pilgrim theme."[99] This position has also been adopted by I. Howard Marshall, who connects the verse with the thematic concept of "the vigor of hope,"[100] as well as by Cross, who connects this with the Paschal Lamb.[101] If verse 13a does indeed refer to a scriptural allusion, then the blessing-section could be extended to 1:13a, with only 1:13b remaining

---

thanks to God for the wonderful salvation to be revealed in all fullness at the second coming of Christ, Peter now urges his readers to conduct which is in accord with their high privileges and glorious destiny." This interpretation is not a new one, for even The Venerable Bede (*Commentary on the Seven Catholic Epistles*, 77) understood 1:13 as building upon the preceding discussion, with a shift toward human conduct.

[99]Hillyer, *1 and 2 Peter, Jude*, 44: "The Greek is literally 'gird up the loins of your mind' (as KJV), a vivid metaphor of the Eastern worker prepared for action, having hitched up his flowing robe so as not to be impeded. The people of Israel had been told to celebrate the Passover in this fashion, to show that they were ready to go forward (Exod. 12:11). This event may well be at the back of Peter's mind, for exodus symbolism underlies the whole of this section (vv. 13-21). There is a promised land ahead!" Davids (*The First Epistle of Peter*, 66) is not as confident as some in seeing a scriptural allusion in 1:13a, claiming that "Peter *might* also have been *influenced* by Exod. 12:11 . . ." [emph. mine]. Cranfield (*The First Epistle of Peter*, 32; see also his, *1 & II Peter and Jude*, 47) sees 1:13a as an example of humour being used by the Petrine author.

[100]Marshall, *1 Peter*, 51: "The language can in fact be traced back to Exodus 12:11 where the Israelites, about to leave Egypt, are told to eat the Passover, dressed and equipped to start out on the long and tough journey without delay. So too Peter's readers are to set out on their journey to the 'Promised Land' and must be ready for action. To go out as Christians on pilgrimage through the world demands vigor."

[101]Cross, *1 Peter: A Paschal Liturgy*, 24-26, sees 1:13 as a reference to Exodus 12:11, arguing for references to the Paschal Lamb throughout 1 Peter (e.g. 1:18; 1:13; 2:9; and 2:11) -- indeed, for Cross (25) this Paschal Lamb theme functions as the underlying concept for 1:13-21. Thus, for Cross the Exodus deliverance is a key typological tale for 1 Peter and "for the Christian Church the leading Old Testament type of Easter" (24).

within the body-opening. The use of scriptural quotations or allusions to conclude a section has been clearly established in Petrine scholarship.[102] If this applies to 1:13, however, then the letter formula of a body-opening falls apart. It would be extremely speculative to force the body-opening to only be comprised of "set all your hope on the grace that Jesus Christ will bring you when he is revealed." The presence of the first imperative ("to hope") in the letter at verse 13 further makes it unlikely that 1:13b fits the blessing. This imperative fits best with the deliberative discourse following the blessing, rather than with the epideictic nature of the Petrine blessing. In other words, the imperative at 1:13 would serve no purpose within the blessing (unlike the body-opening), and thus should not be considered a part of the blessing. Furthermore, as Best has argued, "gird up your minds" is a common metaphor, and, therefore, "there is no need to see dependence of the metaphor on Lk. 12:35 or in any special way on the Exodus event (Exod. 12:11)."[103] Thus, even if 1:13a does parallel Exodus 12:11, the common nature of the metaphor makes it unlikely that the Petrine author consciously drew upon the scriptural source or that the addressees would have interpreted verse 13a as a scriptural allusion. Consequently, 1:13a should not be seen as containing a scriptural allusion to Exodus 12:11. The entirety of verse 13 belongs in the body-opening.

THE TRANSITION FROM BODY OPENING
TO BODY MIDDLE (1:13-14)

The function of the body-opening, as stated above, is to transfer the reader from the blessing-section into the body-middle (1:14-5:11). Furthermore, the

---

[102]Dalton, *Christ's Proclamation to the Spirits*, 76: "The great authority of the Old Testament in the mind of the New Testament writer makes it highly suitable to end off an argument or development of thought with a biblical citation. In this way the thought comes to a sort of impressive climax. The more important and massive the scripture quotation, the more emphatic is the break between this section and the following. Of course, citation of scripture need not necessarily mean the end of a development, but it is quite constantly used to indicate this."

[103]Best, *1 Peter*, 84.

body-opening functions to set the thematic stage for the body-middle. Therefore, 1:13 must function to interrelate, or bridge, the two sections of the letter that border the verse.[104]

> 1:13 -- Διὸ ἀναζωσάμενοι τὰς ὀσφύας τῆς διανοίας ὑμῶν νήφοντες τελείως ἐλπίσατε ἐπὶ τὴν φερομένην ὑμῖν χάριν ἐν ἀποκαλύψει Ἰησοῦ Χριστοῦ.

Therefore prepare your minds for action; discipline yourselves; set all your hope on the grace that Jesus Christ will bring you when he is revealed.

> 1:14 -- ὡς τέκνα ὑπακοῆς μὴ συσχηματιζόμενοι ταῖς πρότερον ἐν τῇ ἀγνοίᾳ ὑμῶν ἐπιθυμίαις.

Like obedient children, do not be conformed to the desires that you formerly had in ignorance.

The author utilizes ὡς in verse 14a to mark the new compositional unit of 1 Peter. It functions to correlate the community's ethical/social conduct with the simile of τέκνα ὑπακοῆς ("children of obedience").[105] This particle clearly creates a definite break with verse 13,[106] as it sets out a new section in which the

---

[104]White (*The Form and Function of the Body of the Greek Letter*, 33): "The body-opening is the point at which the principal occasion for the letter is usually indicated. In addition, the body-opening must proceed, like spoken conversation, from a basis common to both parties. This is provided either by allusion to subject matter shared by both parties or by the addressor's disclosure of new information. The body-opening lays the foundation, in either case, from which the superstructure may grow." Best (*1 Peter*, 84) refers to 1:13 as "a transition verse," which is indicated by "therefore."

[105]Hillyer (*1 and 2 Peter, Jude*, 45) perceives a "Semitic idiom behind the Greek" of "as obedient children." Hillyer also places a great deal of importance on the concept of obedience in 1 Peter -- an emphasis that Hillyer brings out when entering the body of the letter (44-46). On page 47, in his "additional notes," Hillyer states that obedient children means "lit. 'children of obedience,' a common Semitism which points to a particular characteristic; e.g. 2 Sam. 7:10, 'children of wickedness' (KJV) = 'wicked people' (NIV). The Semitism appears elsewhere in the NT (as in Luke 16:8; John 12:36; Eph 2:2-3, 1 Thess 5:5), for while Greek is the language of the NT, most of the writers come from a background of Judaism. In this short letter Peter frequently stresses the vital importance of obedience to God (1:2, 14, 22: 2:13, 18; 3:1, 5, 6; 4:17; 5:5)." Obedience, as a key theme in 1 Peter, has also been recognized by Cranfield (*The First Epistle of Peter*, 34; *I & II Peter and Jude*, 50) and relates to the Christian's submission to God, with a sharp break from "the insidious attractions of the old lusts of their pagan past."

[106]Contra Johnston, *First Epistle of Peter*, 88-89.

correlation ("like") is with what follows the particle, rather than what has preceded this compositional marker. The use of ὡς is in contrast to the use of διό in verse 13a, where a shift, moreso than a sharp break, occurs between sections. Therefore the body-opening is linked with the blessing-section at verse 13, due to the transitional function of the body-opening, which moves the reader/hearer from the blessing into the body-middle. The body-opening (1:13), however, does not use the same transitional device as found in verse 14, to build a connection with the body-middle.

The definite break between verses 13 and 14 is further demonstrated by the eschatological climax in the body-opening: "set all your hope on the grace that Jesus Christ will bring you when he is revealed [ἀποκαλύψει]." The emphasis in this imperatival statement is for the recipients to be hopeful as they move toward the eschatological presence of Christ.[107] The imagery that this statement evokes is of one who is desperately holding onto a hope, and who will (due to being faithful/hopeful) receive a reward at the conclusion of the struggle. In this struggle just prior to the eschaton, the Petrine community is admonished to make this hope a complete commitment (thus, τελείως modifies the imperative and denotes "completeness" or "fullness").[108] Therefore the intensity of this hope is emphasized in this syntactical construction, an intensity that is further emphasized

---

[107]According to Goppelt (*A Commentary on 1 Peter*, 102) the imperatives here are in the aorist and "therefore, they summon the readers not into a condition but to active initiative in various situations. 'Hope' (1:13) does not mean 'have hope,' but 'show that hope has been given to you.' 'Love one another' (1:22) does not mean 'cherish love as an attitude,' but 'show one another brotherly love in every situation.' These two imperatives, together with the present tense imperative in 2:5, which summons the readers to abiding incorporation into the community, announce the themes for the three parts of this section." Consequently, the paraenetical thrust here is an active participation of the recipients in the eschatological process, rather than to be merely passive recipients who stand fast during difficult times. Selwyn (*The First Epistle of St. Peter*, 140), however, claims that the aorist imperative does not serve any special purpose here, but rather "may be little more than a trait of individual style; for, 'in general, the aorist imperative is considered more forcible and urgent than the present.'"

[108]Davids (*The First Epistle of Peter*, 67) is correct in emphasizing the correlation between this eschatological hope and the community situation: "Their hope, however, is not a 'pie-in-the-sky-by-and-by' type of hope isolated from the present world and its concerns, but one that directly controls how they live in the present: they are to live 'as obedient children.'"

by the position of τελείως in the statement prior to ἐλπίσατε.[109] Although the NRSV translates this statement as "set all your hope on . . .," a more emphatic translation would run "FULLY set your hope on . . ."[110] This emphatic translation better articulates the ontological situation of struggling, within which the Petrine community finds itself.[111] In the process of struggling toward the eschaton, the preceding statement (v. 13a) has already expressed the practical approach in holding onto this hope. The recipients are admonished: "prepare your minds for action" and "discipline yourselves." The closing statement, ἐν ἀποκαλύψει Ἰησοῦ Χριστοῦ ("in the revealing of Jesus Christ"), summarily presents the victorious conclusion of this whole "hoping" process/journey. This is surely climactic, and thereby ends the section on a high positive note. Resultant from this climactic rise, the body-opening neatly draws to a definitive conclusion.

The presence of a sharp break between verses 13 and 14 is due to the second purpose of the body-opening, i.e. to set the thematic stage for the body-middle. The ὡς (v. 14) and the ἀλλά (v. 15) function to create an antithetical construction for the sentence that runs from the beginning of verse 14 to the end of verse 16. Whereas verse 14 emphasizes the ethical life to be avoided ("do not be conformed to the desires that you formerly had in ignorance"), verses 15 and 16 exhort an ethic of holiness, which is based upon imitating the holiness of Jesus

---

[109]Goppelt (*A Commentary on 1 Peter*, 107), Selwyn (*The First Epistle of St. Peter*, 140), and Schelkle (*Die Petrusbriefe*, 44) correctly understand τελείως belonging to ἐλπίσατε, rather than νήφοντες (contra Windisch, *Die Katholischen Briefe*, 55; and Beare, *The First Epistle of Peter*, 96). As Selwyn notes: "it is unusual for an adverb to follow the verb which it qualifies . . . and a better sense is given if τελείως is taken with ἐλπίσατε."

[110]Although an adverb will usually follow the verb it qualifies, the emphatic essence is still present given the opening of the new clause within the sentence (this is, of course, assuming a minor break after νήφοντες, rather than after to τελείως). Thus, both the position in relation to the verb and the position in relation to the clause determine the emphatic reading of τελείως -- indeed, the very function of the adverb is to offer a qualifying emphasis to the verb.

[111]In a similar interpretation of τελείως, Lenski (*Interpretation*, 52) understands this adverb as meaning with "finality" (not "perfectly," contra Hort, *The First Epistle of St. Peter*), rendering the sentence as "'set your hope with finality on the grace being brought to you,' i.e. do not set your hope on this grace only tentatively or in a halfhearted way."

Christ.[112] This exhortation is supported by a scriptural quotation, which is used to conclude the subsection (1:14-16). The time factor in this antithesis needs to be noted. The negative side of the antithesis refers back to the recipients' previous life, whereas the positive side states the expected present ethical conduct demanded from the recipients. In other words, the recipients are being admonished to continue forward along the "eschatological journey" toward the eschaton, which is perceived as being imminent, and not to defect from the faith back to their former way of being the non-elect.[113] According to John Piper, the eschatological hope of verse 13 sets forth the basis for the ethical conduct of verses 14-15.[114]

The antithetical thrust here is preceded by the body-opening in order to state thematically, at the very outset, that the recipients are to follow the precept for an ethic of holiness. Thus, from a compositional standpoint, the body-opening functions to connect transitionally the body-middle with the blessing-section. Two different transitional devices are utilized in the process. The first places an emphatic inclusio around the blessing, while the second forces the reader to see the body-opening as an introductory heading for the thematic/paraenetic thrust of the body-middle. The connection between the blessing-section and the body-middle articulates the theme of 1:13a: the recipients' response to the mercy of God. Antithetically the recipients are given a choice of responding either positively (holy ethical conduct), or negatively (a rejection of God's mercy and a

---

[112]Beare (*The First Epistle of Peter*, 97) indicates that κατά (v. 15) is used "in the sense of moral conformity to a model."

[113]This "eschatological journey" motif is developed and used by Martin, *Metaphor and Composition in 1 Peter*, passim. A similar usage of time can be found in the antithetical presentation of the believers' previous and present condition in *Interpretation of Knowledge* 9,27-38. It is my position that the *Interp. Know.* is also a paraenetic text (or at least this pericope) intended to encourage (Valentinian) Christians not to defect from their faith (I hope to demonstrate the paraenetic nature of the *Interp. Know.* in a future study on paraenesis in Valentinianism).

[114]John Piper, "Hope as the Motivation of Love: 1 Peter 3:9-12," *NTS* 26 (1980): 215.

return to the way of ignorance).[115] The time factor, of which verse 13 agrees with verses 15-16 in expected present conduct, determines that the recipients are admonished to respond to this mercy in the positive. Thus, a thematic "flow" can be observed running from the blessing-section through the body-opening into the body-middle.

---

[115]According to Hillyer (*1 and 2 Peter, Jude*, 47) ignorance here holds a relational connotation: "**Ignorance** in Jewish terminology meant more than a lack of knowledge. It characterized those who did not know the true God. The choice of word may imply that many of Peter's readers were from a pagan background (cf. 1:18; 2:10, 25; 4:3), but on at least one occasion he brought the same charges against Jews (Acts 3:17)." In interpreting 1 Peter 1:22 as "through the living and enduring word of God," Eugene A. LaVerdiere ("A Grammatical Ambiguity in 1 Pet 1:23," *CBQ* 36 [1974]: 89-94) observes the shift to the practical concerns of Christian life "on how regeneration constitutes a continuing basis for a Christian attitude" (94).

CHAPTER THREE:
CONCLUSION

This study has focused upon the introductory sections of 1 Peter. By looking at the Petrine prescript, we have discovered that the author programmatically modified epistolary formulae in designing 1:1-2 in order to set forth the thematic and compositional basis for the rest of the letter. This is important for understanding the author's rhetorical strategy. That is, the author of 1 Peter wished to present the Petrine community as ontologically separated from their earthly existence, and, therefore, referred to them as "exiles" of the "dispersion." The various provincial territories mentioned further heighten this diaspora condition. The disenfranchised status of the recipients is to be understood as the essence of the community's perceived "persecuted"/"suffering" condition. This condition is, furthermore, to be understood in light of the closing formula of verse 2, i.e. their ontological status in relation to God.

The transitional flow from the prescript's conclusion into the opening of the blessing continues the rhetorical purpose of the prescript. The opening of the blessing (1:3) and the closing of the prescript (1:2) are separated by a sharp break, representing a definite compositional shift. This shift, however, also includes a movement from the grace given (1:2) to the source of that grace (1:3-5). Thus, the blessing's "call to worship" is one of epideictic praise and adoration for what God, through Jesus Christ, has accomplished. Here we find the rhetorical strategy of suppression working well. The author has not dwelt on the negative aspects of the diaspora status of community, but rather has emphasized the positive aspects of being part of the Christian diaspora. This praiseful tone dominates the entirety of the blessing-section.

The blessing concludes with an eschatological climax (1:10-12). The climax includes an allusion to the Jewish scriptures, albeit in a very general sense. The closing of the blessing presents the current status of the Petrine Christians within the broader framework of God's soteriological drama. In the author's view they were, in essence, part of the climactic eschatological fulfillment of the greatest drama ever to be conceived.[1]   The climax is one in which the entire prophetic enterprise looked forward in anticipation, and which the angelic realm also looked upon in awe and wonder.   In effect, this salvation history is a process of increasing glorification.   The Petrine community was to rejoice over their diaspora condition, for they also participated in this glory.   The sufferings and glories of Christ are paradigmatic for Christians. As Schutter has emphasized, the sufferings-glories schema of 1:10-12 serves as the hermeneutical key for the way the Petrine author has utilized scripture.[2]   This same schema is fundamental for understanding the consolatory thrust of 1 Peter. The Petrine author presents Christ as the archetype of Christians' eschatological journey: As Christ suffered and attained glory, so also will Christians, for in fact Christians now embrace the suffering/glory of Christ.

The body-opening, which comprises 1:13 entirely, is closely connected to the preceding verses.   Through the simple transitional device διό ("therefore"), the author creates an intimate connection between the body-opening and the blessing. This non-definite compositional break declares that the blessing serves as the introductory basis on which the following exhortations are based. A shift from epideictic (1:3-12) to deliberative discourse (1:13) occurs. Noteworthy is the presence of the first imperative in 1 Peter. Although it would be pushing the issue too far to argue that "hope" is the controlling theme of the letter, or of the first metaphor cluster, ἐλπίσατε ("hope") does play a key role in the rhetorical strategy of 1 Peter. The theme of hope is closely connected to the rhetorical strategy of suppression. The connection with the eschatological nature of 1:10-12 highlights that, due to this suffering/glory schema, the Petrine community is to have "hope," which results in their obediently carrying out the following

---

[1]First Peter's eschatological presentation does not fit the Jewish apocalyptic genre. As Goppelt so well put it: "It is decisive that 1 Peter defines eschatological salvation not, according to the thought structure of Jewish apocalyptic literature, as the end of history (II Esdr. 7:30f.), but 'salvation-historically' as the fulfillment of prophecy." Thus, 1 Peter is eschatological, but not apocalyptic.

[2]Schutter, *Hermeneutic and Composition in 1 Peter*, 123.

exhortation(s). Thus, the transitional movement from the blessing to the body-opening is one from praise to response.

An inclusio of prescript-blessing-opening was also discerned in this study. The shift from the condition of the community to a focus on the divine, and then a further shift back to the community in response, places an added emphasis on the blessing. The letter-opening's introductory nature is again emphasized. The rhetorical impact of these compositional shifts is to persuade the Petrine community to focus their attention upon the glory of God, of which they also are participating in, rather than upon the negative status that these Christians perceive themselves as holding within society. This is all closely aligned with the diaspora condition of the community and the consolatory intention of the Petrine author.[3]

The body-opening functions as a compositional-transitional-unit which is intended to bridge and, thereby, interrelate the blessing and the body-middle.[4] In the analysis of the transition from the body-opening to the body-middle, it was noted that a definite, sharp, compositional break is made between 1:13 and 1:14. The body-opening served as the introductory "header" for the three metaphor clusters of the body-middle. The shift toward hortatory devices, specifically the presence of the first imperative in 1 Peter, signified the shift from the prescript-blessing, where a discussion of the grace given is heralded with eschatological praise, to the paraenetical direction of the letter, where the socioreligious implications of the letter-opening are discussed. This aspect of the transitional

---

[3]It is typically a difficult task to ascertain the *intention* of an author, due to the dangers of subjectivity interfering with objective reading. Indeed, the very process of "reading" a text creates an interactive relationship between the reader and the writer so as to make a purely objective understanding of authorial intention highly suspect. Despite this methodological difficulty, the material presented in this book offers a high degree of plausibility to an exegetical unraveling of the Petrine author's rhetorical agenda. Indeed, it is through ascertaining the rhetorical strategy of a text that a plausible (albeit indirect) understanding of authorial intention can be derived.

[4]John Hurd (*The Origin of 1 Corinthians*, 2nd ed. [Macon, GA: Mercer University Press, 1983 (1965)], 89-90). has similiarly identified the role of transitional units in 1 Corinthians. He identifies 1 Corinthians 6:12-20 as "a transitional passage [intended] to conclude his [Paul's] treatment of oral information and to introduce his answers to the Corinthians' questions" (89). Cf. *Rhetorica Ad Herennium* 4.26.35 for a brief discussion on transitions.

flow from the blessing to the body-middle via the body-opening substantiates the introductory nature of the letter-opening.

This present compositional study of 1 Peter's letter-opening aids in assessing certain key issues in Petrine studies. One such issue is eschatology. The eschatological nature of 1 Peter has long been observed. Within this study, it has been observed that an eschatological thrust is utilized to conclude such transitional sections as 1:10-12. The same can be said for the transition from 3:12 to 3:13, as well as at 2:10. An eschatological climax has the rhetorical function of concluding one section with an elevated emphasis, which would thereby offer eschatological hope to the Petrine community.

As argued by Robert L. Webb, 1 Peter's eschatological theme can be understood as a form of eclectic apocalypticism, even though 1 Peter is not strictly an apocalypse in literary form.[5] Webb argues that 1 Peter's eschatological matrix contains a temporal axis, a chronologically oriented apocalyptic eschatology where a strong emphasis is placed upon protology, specifically the primordial events such as the Noachic type in 3:18-22, and a spatial axis, i.e. a cosmological demarcation between otherwordly regions and otherwordly beings, as well as the relations between them. Davids has developed Webb's insights and has seen a strong eschatological flow in 1 Peter.[6] Within discussions of Petrine eschatology the issue of time has played a significant role. Does 1 Peter emphasize a realized eschatology, a future eschatology, or even a melding of the two? Recently, David C. Parker has argued for a strong realized eschatological perspective in 1 Peter. In summation of his study of 1:4b-5, 1:7, 1:13, 2:12, 4:13, and 5:1, Parker states that "the writer is attempting to set out a way of Christian life whose foundation is the character of God's act in Christ, and the character of Christ's life." Therefore, Parker emphasizes that

---

[5]Webb, "The Apocalyptic Perspective of First Peter," 15-24.

[6]Davids, *The First Epistle of Peter*, 15-17.

> [in] the verses we have been examining, the important thing, from which is developed an interpretation of the Christian life and suffering as revelation, is that the Christian has been reborn by God into this living hope, a world in which the glory shines from the beginning, the resurrection of Jesus Christ from the dead.[7]

Although Parker has correctly perceived the significance of present time within Petrine eschatology, his method, and thus his specific exegetical work, is highly questionable. His study is based upon a running debate with five modern translations (Good News Bible, New International Version, New Jerusalem Bible, New Revised Standard Version, and Revised English Bible) and a selection of commentators. Little grammatical or syntactical analysis is applied to the verses selected. Furthermore, Parker fails to consider the contextual framework within which these eschatological statements function. Consequently, his proposed translations, all of which follow his understanding of Petrine eschatology, suffer from a lack of substantiation.

In understanding the eschatological nature of 1 Peter, the time reference is best understood as a correlation between both present and future eschatological perspectives.[8] According to Martin, the Petrine author has presented a past-present-future eschatology -- specifically in relation to the ontological condition, or rhetorical situation, of the community.[9] The Petrine conception of the present and the future can be seen as being so closely interwoven that the future is the imminent transformation (or fulfillment) of the present. This motif is, in essence, a consolatory technique used by the Petrine author to alleviate the (perceived or real) oppression of the recipients. As Webb clearly states:

---

[7]David C. Parker, "The Eschatology of 1 Peter," *BTB* 24 (1994): 31.

[8]A similar present-future eschatological reading of 1 Peter was taken by Selwyn ("Eschatology in 1 Peter," in eds. W. Davies and D. Daube, *The Background of the New Testament and its Eschatology: In Honour of Charles Harold Dodd* [Cambridge: Cambridge University Press, 1964], 394-401).

[9]Martin, *Metaphor and Composition in 1 Peter*, 274.

Therefore, for these readers the time of eschatological salvation is the revelation of Jesus Christ at the Eschaton. This hope was intensified by imminency of the eschatological event. They expected their Savior's revelation and their salvation within their own lifetime.[10]

The eschatological base of 1 Peter, consequently, is best seen as closely related to the rhetorical strategy of the Petrine author to encourage his recipients. The eschatological imminence of this Petrine theme creates an overlapping relationship between the past, present, and future.

Martin has offered a solid, albeit indirect, grammatical argument for this eschatological interpretation. In arguing that "the present tense verb ἀγαλλιᾶσθε [1:6, 8] is indeed used with future meaning,"[11] he has highlighted the correlative relationship between present and future time reference in 1 Peter, specifically the Petrine blessing. The suggestion that the eschatological nature of 1 Peter interweaves the present and future together is not new, for in 1957 Cross held such a position. He stated as follows:

> It is not a case of a future joy which awaits the Christian as a compensation in the next world. It is a "joy unspeakable" (χαρᾶ ἀνεκλαλήτος) already present. It is unnecessary after the studies of Professors C. H. Dodd and Oscar Cullmann to stress how readily this coexistence of future and present found a place in the eschatological thought of the early Church.[12]

For Cross "the eschatological structure of the thought [in the letter], with its close inter-penetration of future hope and present realization"[13] is evidence of the early nature of 1 Peter (prior to Justin and contemporanous with the rest of the New Testament writings). Regardless of the role that a present-future eschatology may

---

[10]Webb, "The Apocalyptic Perspective of First Peter," 202.

[11]Martin, "The Present Indicative in the Eschatological Statements of 1 Peter 1:6, 8," 312.

[12]Cross, *1 Peter: A Paschal Liturgy*, 23.

[13]Cross, *1 Peter: A Paschal Liturgy*, 43.

serve in the dating of 1 Peter, this motif surely served the rhetorical function of placing the Petrine Christians within the eschatological climax of the soteriological drama (1:10-12) so that their present condition of suffering would appear as only a brief transitory step into eschatological fulfillment or glorification. Indeed, the closeness of the present to the future makes future hopes seem already a part of the present reality.[14] In regard to the eschatological present-future relationship in 1 Peter, Kendall has argued that the future connotation of "hope" is closely connected in 1 Peter to the present condition of the Petrine community. Thus, the eschatological hope in 1 Peter is a consolatory theme.[15] Rhetorically this motif serves to encourage the Petrine community along their own eschatological journey.

The transitional motion within 1 Peter's compositional structure, as evidenced in this present study, functions to bring this eschatological form of encouragement into the forefront of the climactical conclusions of the various sections of 1 Peter. Within the blessing the compositional transition's eschatological thrust (1:10-12) serves to raise the Petrine community's perspective that their glorification is imminent. Thus, the transitions serve as key elements within the eschatological strategy of the Petrine author.

Another key issue within Petrine studies is the issue of compositional integrity. As outlined in the history of scholarship section of this book, the form critical approach to 1 Peter raised serious questions as to the unity of the text, arguing instead for various partition and source critical theories. Martin's compositional study of 1 Peter, like Dalton's before him, substantiated the unity of the letter. Martin's study attempted to tie all the metaphorical units together with the diaspora metaphor. By arguing that the literary units in 1 Peter are generated and controlled by one metaphorical motif, Martin helps to highlight the

---

[14]It is important to also note the interplay of eschatology and ethics in 1 Peter's paraenetic presentation. For a brief survey of this interplay, see Ronald Russell, "Eschatology and Ethics in 1 Peter," *EvQ* 47 (1975): 78-84.

[15]Kendall, "1 Peter 1:3-9. On Christian Hope," passim. See also Achtemeier, "Newborn Babes and Living Stones," 231-35.

rhetorically unified argument of the letter and, thereby, the unified nature of that argument. Petrine studies has seen a rising consensus in accepting the compositional integrity of 1 Peter.[16] This book has assisted in building the argument for compositional integrity. By looking at the transitional motion within the letter opening, we are better able to see the interwoven nature of the various compositional units. The rhetorical strategy of 1 Peter is developed as the Petrine author moved from one section of the letter into the next. Thus, the integrity of the text has been further substantiated.

The rhetorical sophistication of 1 Peter is closely aligned with the compositional movement of the letter. Thus, this present study of the compositional transitions in 1 Peter's letter-opening aids in underscoring the interwoven nature of the rhetorical strategy of 1 Peter and the letter's compositional flow. The eschatological web and the rhetorical strategy of suppression also highlight this aspect of the document. What is needed now is to extend this study to the compositional transitions throughout the rest of 1 Peter, so as to fully ascertain the role of the compositional transitions in 1 Peter. It is our hope that this study has provided a useful foundation to such a comprehensive study.

---

[16]See, for example, Martin, *Metaphor and Composition in 1 Peter*; Dalton, *Christ's Proclamation to the Spirits*; Schutter, *Hermeneutic and Composition in 1 Peter*; Davids, *The First Epistle of Peter*; Thurén, *The Rhetorical Strategy of 1 Peter*; Kistemaker, *Exposition on the Epistles of Peter*, 24; Goppelt, *A Commentary on 1 Peter*; Kendall, "The Literary and Theological Function of 1 Peter 1:3-12"; Webb, "The Apocalyptic Perspective of First Peter"; Glenny, "The Hermeneutics of the the Use of the Old Testament in 1 Peter"; Achtemeier, "Newborn Babes and Living Stones"; Tite, "The Compositional Function of the Petrine Prescript"; Pearson, "The Christological Hymnic Pattern of 1 Peter"; R. P. Martin, *The Theology of the Letters of James, Peter, and Jude*; and Slaughter, "The Importance of the Literary Argument for Understanding 1 Peter."

APPENDIX 1:

A MODIFICATION OF THE FIRST METAPHOR CLUSTER:

Οἶκος-CLUSTER (1:14-2:10)

Martin's compositional analysis of the first metaphor cluster perceives the dominating metaphor as the "elect household of God." From this controlling metaphor, the passage divides into two sub-sections of metaphors: (1) οἶκος-metaphors arising from the new birth and consequent familial relations (1:14-25), which then sub-divides into three metaphors of obedient children (1:14-16), reverence (1:17-21), and brotherly love (1:22-25); (2) οἶκος-metaphors arising from the conception of growth (2:1-10), which is comprised of two groups of metaphors of newborn babes/spiritual milk (2:1-3) and living stones/new Temple metaphors (2:4-10). All the metaphors in this passage, according to Martin, emerge from the general metaphor of the elect household of God. The second group of metaphors is a natural development from the preceding set (from familial relations to growth). Although Martin has correctly identified the metaphors that comprise this passage, he has overemphasized the "household" element of the controlling metaphor. The metaphor of "election" by itself more accurately stands as the controlling metaphor for this first cluster. The presence of the οἶκος aspect of the metaphors functions to correlate (interpretatively) the two sets of "election" metaphors. These two sections better divide into two topoi of "οἶκος as familial" and "οἶκος as priestly." Furthermore, as will be brought out below, the division between these two independent οἶκος sections does not lie at 2:1, but rather at 2:4. The transitional function of 2:1-3 is the key to understanding the compositional motion within this metaphor cluster. Consequently, a brief

81

excursus, albeit still relevant to understanding the compositional transitions in 1 Peter, from the major transitional breaks in the letter is in order.

The conceptual development of the first metaphor cluster is closely related to a dual meaning of οἶκος. Martin is correct in demonstrating that οἶκος "carries a double meaning, both of which provide material for the metaphors in this section of the body-middle . . . in one sense οἶκος refers to the house or building that provided living quarters for the family" and therefore being in relation to God "qualifies a Temple";[1] and secondly οἶκος refers to the family that constituted the household, including the privileges and obligations of those members. In pulling these two concepts of οἶκος together, Martin states:

> This conception of the οἶκος as a family composed of members who have specific roles and responsibilities along with the conception of οἶκος as a house dominates the constellation of metaphors in this first section of the body-middle of 1 Peter.[2]

Within the Jewish and Christian traditions, the idea of a "household" referring to the people of God prevailed within most of the literature of the first and second centuries.[3] Indeed, to view the Temple as the "house" of God, which functions as the central point of community identification, was a key theme within this period -- both before and after the destruction of Jerusalem.[4] The diaspora mentality, and the idea of οἶκος as the people of God, goes back as far as the exile.[5] Within the Judaism of the Greco-Roman world, the Temple, as the "house

---

[1]Martin, *Metaphor and Composition in 1 Peter*, 165.

[2]Martin, *Metaphor and Composition in 1 Peter*, 167.

[3]A fascinating example of this tendency can be found in the *Shepherd of Hermas*, where an interplay between Hermas' family (household) and the church is present and, thus, the correlation of Hermas with the leadership of the community of faith and the household as metaphorical of that community. This is present throughout the text, as it is a running theme throughout the *Shepherd*.

[4]See R. J. McKelvey, *The New Temple: The Church in the New Testament*, Oxford Theology Monographs (Oxford: Oxford University Press, 1969), 42-57.

[5]Cf. Causse, *Les dispersés d'Israël*, 31-34.

of God," served as the central point of Jewish identity.[6] Indeed, even with the diversity of the Jewish people of this period -- scholars now tend to refer to Judaisms rather than Judaism -- the Temple served as a symbolic point of coherence to offer this people a sense of unity and restorational hopes. The destruction of the Temple, subsequently, generated a near catastrophic paradigm shift within the Jewish conscience itself. Christianity, as a form of first century Jewish plurality, did not escape this paradigmatic crisis.

According to Troy Martin, the first metaphor cluster includes a series of metaphors that are related to "growth."[7] These metaphors run from 2:1-10. Martin refers to them as "Metaphor-Newborn Babies" (2:1-3) and "Metaphor-Living Stones" (2:4-10). This group of metaphors follows a series of metaphors related directly to the concept of οἶκος as "family." The closing metaphors are seen as an obvious development of the "family household" theme that dominates this metaphor cluster. The difficulty with Martin's compositional breakdown, however, lies in the clear shift that occurs between the οἶκος-newbirth metaphors running from the opening of this cluster to 2:3 and the οἶκος-Temple/Living Stones metaphors of the closing section of the first metaphor cluster.

Martin seems to force the closing metaphor set into the context of the first set of metaphors. Although they are both related to the concept of οἶκος, they are slightly more distinct than Martin would imply. Indeed, the "growth" metaphors of 2:1-3 more closely relate to the metaphors in the "οἶκος-metaphors arising from the new birth and consequent familial relations (1:14-25)."[8] There is the concept of children arising in 1:14 at the very outset, and then picked up

---

[6]See Menahem Haran, "Temple and Community in Ancient Israel," in Michael V. Fox, ed., *Temple in Society* (Winona Lake, MN: Eisenbrauns, 1988), 17-25.

[7]The theme of "growth" beginning at 2:1 is not original with Martin. Demarest (*Commentary on the Catholic Epistles*, 193, 197-98), for example, also interpreted these metaphors with a very strong "growth" theme. Further, see Benson (*A Paraphrase*, 205) who also sees the Temple as "growing" from the foundation stone; and Miller, "Deliverance and Destiny," 419-21.

[8]Martin, *Metaphor and Composition in 1 Peter*, 187 gives an outline of this first metaphor cluster. This is the sectional title he gives to this first group of metaphors in this cluster.

again at 2:2 just prior to the "living stones" discussion. Between these two references, the author outlines familial relations in parallel with the Petrine Christians' relationship with God (note the terms "father," "inherited," "ancestors," and the repetition of "obedience" from 1:14 in 1:22 -- all of which denote familial relations). Thus, a sectional inclusio is best seen between 1:14 and 2:3, constructed with the designations τέκνα (1:14) and ἀρτιγέννητα βρέφη (2:2),[9] with 2:3 merely being a closing comment on 2:2 (note the εἰ).[10] The thematic concept of God's creative activity (i.e., a "birthing" process) is nicely presented within this inclusio.[11] Therefore, Martin's inclusion of 2:1-3 in the "living stones"

---

[9]The inclusio of τέκνα (1:14) and ἀρτιγέννητα βρέφη (2:2) is preferable over the suggested inclusio of χάριν ἐν ἀποκαλύψει Ἰησοῦ Χριστοῦ (1:13) and χρηστός (2:3) by Glenny ("The Hermeneutics of the Use of the Old Testament in 1 Peter," 331). Glenny does not recognize the role of 1:13 as the body-opening, and consequently draws an inclusio between two terms which do not belong within the same compositional unit. This typifies Glenny's entire compositional proposal (329-42), where he does not apply epistolary formulae to 1 Peter despite the fact that he identifies 1 Peter as a unified epistle (326-27, 340-41). Furthermore, the similarity in sound between these terms is not as clear and distinct as Glenny believes. Nor, for that matter, do they correlate with the dominate themes of this compositional unit. This even applies to Glenny's view that in 1:13-2:3 "Peter exhorts his readers as the children of God (1:14, 17, 23; 2:2)" (331). Thus, although Glenny is correct in identifying a minor break between 2:3 and 2:4, he is incorrect in his argumentation.

[10]Although most manuscripts have εἰ, some have εἴπερ (א[c] C K P Ψ 049 056 0142 [33 εἴσπερ] 81 88 104 181 326 330 436 451 614 629 630 945 1241 1505 1739 1877 1881 2412 2492 2495 Byx Lect it[ar,c,dem,p,(z)] vg syr[h] Cyril Ps-Oecumenius Theophylact), and only one has ὅπερ (Byzantine lectionary; l[1590] -- 13th century). The variation is not significant for the meaning of this verse. As Glenny ("The Hermeneutics of the Use of the Old Testament in 1 Peter") states, "the sense of the passage is not changed regardless of the particle used since εἰ with the indicative assumes or implies that the statement is true" (103, ftn. 88). Glenny prefers, however, to see εἰ as the best reading: "The major textual problem is the choice between εἰ and εἴπερ. Because εἴπερ is used nowhere else in the New Testament outside of Paul's writings, because εἰ has good early support (p[72], א, A, B) and because the manuscripts that read εἴπερ (א[2], C, P, Ψ, M) appear to emphasize the definiteness or certainty of the statement, εἰ is accepted as the original reading" (103). Furthermore, the author's use of ἐγεύσασθε ("to taste" or "to partake") in 2:3 is a clear reference to the "spiritual milk" metaphor of 2:2. The Venerable Bede correctly understands 2:1-2 as reflecting back to the new birth motif (Commentary on the Seven Catholic Epistles, 80). Even Cranfield (The First Epistle of Peter, 44), who groups 2:1-10 together under the thematic title "The People of God," has recognized that the "spiritual milk" metaphor of 2:2 best relates back to the "newborn babes" metaphor of 1:3, 23.

[11]Beare (The First Epistle of Peter, 114) notes this in his discussion of the newbirth imagery in this passage: "'newborn babes' -- in strict literalness 'newly-begotten embryos'. The writer consistently thinks of the new life of the Christian in terms not of birth, but of begetting; the creative action of God as Father is never out of his mind. . . . The true meaning of βρέφος is 'embryo' (always used with this meaning in Homer), not 'babe'; but in the usage of later writers it is extended to include sucklings and even small children generally (=νήπιος). The craving for milk is of course a figure that would

metaphor group (due to dealing with growth or building-up) should be modified.[12] Instead, Goppelt's division between the "new birth section" and the "stone motif" should be followed, where 2:4 marks the second sub-section of this first section.[13]

In his own study, Martin offers support to this evaluation of seeing 2:4 as the key break within the metaphor cluster. He states that 2:4-10 "is introduced by a conjunctive participial phrase in verse four and concluded by extended scripture quotation and midrash in verses 6-10."[14] Although Martin identifies this conjunctive participial phrase as a minor transitional marker within a sub-section, it is best to understand this transitional marker as indicating the beginning of the second sub-section. Again, Martin states that "because of the relative pronoun ὅν in verse 4, the passage that contains the metaphor of living stones is grammatically subordinate and dependent upon the passage that contains the metaphor of newborn babies."[15] Yet the presence of this relative pronoun, and its subordinating function, does not (contra Martin) indicate 2:4-10 as a continuation

---

be applicable only to the infant, but enough of the original sense remains to make possible the use of the adjective ἀρτιγέννητα -- 'newly-begotten'." Beare applies this metaphor to a baptismal setting. See, however, the non-baptismal argument by J. Francis ("'Like Newborn Babes' -- The Image of the Child in 1 Peter 2:2-3," in *Studia Biblica 1978: III. Papers on Paul and Other New Testament Authors. Sixth International Congress on Biblical Studies, Oxford 3-7 April 1978*, ed. E. A. Livingstone, 111-17, JSNTSup. 3 [Sheffield: JSOT Press, 1980]).

[12]Lenski (*Interpretation*, 76) supplies further evidence for drawing the compositional break at 2:4 rather than 2:1, when he observes that "οὖν adds this admonition as being one that accords with what has just been said in 1:23-25 about our having been begotten again by means of God's living an abiding Word."

[13]Goppelt, *A Commentary on 1 Peter*, 128-34. For Goppelt, the first section of 1 Peter runs from 1:3 to 2:10. Goppelt's understanding of the blessing-section, however, does not distinguish the blessing from the first section of the letter. Rather, he understands the blessing as thematically tied into the first section, and, therefore, compositionally a subsection of the first major section of 1 Peter. Davids (*The First Epistle of Peter*, 85) also recognizes 2:4 as marking a shift in the letter "from that of nourishment to that of security and honor," with πρὸς ὅν προσερχόμενοι λίθον ζῶντα "both introduc[ing] the stone imagery that will dominate the next five verses and designates Christ not as a monument or dead principle, but as the living, resurrected, and therefore life-giving one." Also see Weiss, *A Commentary on the New Testament*, 272.

[14]Martin, *Metaphor and Composition in 1 Peter*, 175.

[15]Martin, *Metaphor and Composition in 1 Peter*, 176-77.

of the "new birth" metaphor. Rather, the two sections are being intimately interconnected by ὅν within the larger context of the cluster's controlling metaphor of "election."[16]

The actual subordination of 2:4-10 to 1:14-2:3 is not due to the second part of the cluster being a development from the "newbirth" metaphors, but rather is evidence of the role of οἶκος to create a topological unity for the entire cluster, so as best to articulate the Petrine community's elect status.[17]   This creates developmental motion in the text -- not surprising, for the theme of development/progress (growth and building) is a natural development from the preceding section.[18]   The usage of the οἶκος theme in this cluster establishes a linkage between "election-new birth" and "election-priestly function." A key tool in topological construction is the usage of linking words. This is present in 1:14-2:10. Within the second part of this cluster the theme of growth/development is preceded by the "spiritual milk" of 2:2. Similarly, the reference to being "holy, for I am holy" at 1:15 presents the holiness theme of οἶκος as a link between the first and second parts, even though this specific aspect of election is dominant in the second part. In effect, there is an anticipatory literary technique being used in the cluster to tie all the elements. The subordination of the second section

---

[16]As Cranfield notes (*I & II Peter and Jude*, 27), elect is a "theme-word of the Epistle (cf. 2.4, 6, 9; 5.13)" beginning with the prescript.

[17]The two sections of this metaphor cluster are thematically separate, with 1:14-2:3 emphasizing familial ("newbirth") aspects of election, while 2:4-10 embarks upon a "building-stone" motif. Consequently, Beare is correct in refuting Perdelwitz' theory (*Die Mysterienreligion*, 69-70) of the "milk" and "stone" metaphors correlating with ancient mystery-cults (Phrygian mother-goddess), where the stone image of fertility (the breasts) was connected with the cup of milk given to initiates. Beare (*The First Epistle of Peter*, 121) states, contra Perdelwitz, that "this line of interpretation is not convincing; for the Stone in the figure is not an image, but a building-stone" and therefore "the transition from the figure of the 'Milk' to that of the 'Stone' is abrupt" in 1 Peter.

[18]Cf. Bennett, *The General Epistles*, 207.

merely highlights the progressive nature of the whole passage. This progressive nature fits well with the rhetorical motion of any persuasive argument.[19]

The subordination of one section to another is not unexpected in 1 Peter, for the author typically builds upon the previous elements/sections of the letter as the document progresses. Indeed, it is this progressive element that has led several to perceive 1 Peter's compositional outline as fluid and therefore not strictly structured.[20] The function of 2:2-3, however, is to be a special compositional unit for structuring this cluster. It is a transitional segment in its entirety (similar to the body-opening). While 2:2-3 concludes the "new birth" metaphor section (and more appropriately belongs with that section), it also presents the developmental theme that the second section of the cluster articulates. Thus, it is a compositional-transitional-unit that interconnects two independent groups of metaphors, with 2:4 forcing the second group of metaphors into a subordinate role of developing upon the first metaphor group.[21] Like the body-

---

[19]Kennedy (*New Testament Interpretation through Rhetorical Criticism*, 5) refers to rhetorical discourse as originating "in speech and its primary product is a speech act, not a text." The oral nature of rhetoric, which is manifested in texts, results in a progressive flow as the discourse is given. Kennedy states the matter as follows: "A speech is linear and cumulative, and any context in it can only be perceived in contrast to what has gone before, especially what has immediately gone before, though a very able speaker lays the ground for what he intends to say later and has a total unity in mind when he first begins to speak."

[20]This position has been most recently articulated by Davids (*The First Epistle of Peter*, 28) who states: "Peter surely did not write with an outline before him. He feels free to merge ideas together through gradual transition rather than through careful distinction. However, he does have a structure."

[21]Cranfield (*The First Epistle of Peter*, 43-45; *I & II Peter and Jude*, 59-62) has recognized that 2:1-3 "form the transition from chapter 1, gathering up the preceding exhortation and preparing the way for what follows" and thereby refers to 2:1-3 as a "transitional exhortation" (*I & II Peter and Jude*, 59). Verse 3 functions to summarize and transition with a double effect: First, 2:3 reflects back onto the preceding discussion of "newbirth," and secondly it looks forward to the following metaphors of 2:4-10 (i.e. as a consequence of this newbirth, "here is the way to prove that you really have tasted . . ." [*I & II Peter and Jude*, 62]). Thus, the compositional-transitional-unit of 1 Peter 2:1-3 functions in a similar fashion as the compositional-transitional-unit of 1:13 -- i.e. both reflect backward and forward, so as to interconnect two literary sections of the document. See also Lenski (*Interpretation*, 82), who says that "a new line of thought is begun: From the idea of babes who merely receive the beneficent care of the Lord, Peter advances, with imagery that is entirely different, to living stones in a spiritual house, yea, to holy, royal priests who render acceptable sacrifice. Yet by starting this new line of thought with a relative clause Peter indicates that this and the preceding paragraphs belong together."

opening, which is also a compositional-transitional-unit, an imperative is present at 2:2. Indeed, "this command to 'desire' or 'long-for' is the only imperative in the passage, the previous phrase having set the stage for it and the following clauses explaining what it means."[22] Therefore, the compositional transition within the first metaphor cluster is best drawn at 2:4.

Due to his different reading of the compositional relationship between 1:14-2:3 and 2:4-10, Martin arrives at a different conclusion concerning the controlling metaphor for binding these two sections together. As stated above, the second set of metaphors does not fit well with the "household" theme. To put the "Temple" metaphors under the same οἶκος banner as the "new birth" metaphors as Martin has done, is to create a forced connection. It is important, therefore, to look for another controlling metaphor for this first cluster than "the elect household of God."

Both of these groups of metaphors in this passage correlate with the theme of divine election. The "new birth" metaphors emphasize the familial relationship that occurs with being the elect people of God. Martin, therefore, correctly sees divine election within this first section. The second set of metaphors also correlates with the theme of divine election. Here, however, the concept of election is more closely related to the Temple cult of ancient Israel.[23] The Levitical understanding of holiness/sanctification as being set apart for a sacred purpose best suits these metaphors, where the Temple is being built up "into a spiritual house, to be a holy priesthood, to offer spiritual sacrifices acceptable to God through Jesus Christ" (2:5). Rather than being the elect "family" of God, the second set of metaphors presents the community of faith as fulfilling the priestly

---

[22]Davids, *The First Epistle of Peter*, 81. Davids notes that of the 23 imperatives in 1 Peter, the only ones to fall outside 2:11-4:10 are at 1:13, 22; 2:2; 4:13, 15, 16; 5:2, 8, 9.

[23]For an overview of the Temple cult, see Menahem Haran, *Temples and Temple-Service in Ancient Israel: An Inquiry into the Character of Cult Phenomena and the Historical Setting of the Priestly School* (Oxford: Clarendon Press, 1978); and Bertil Gärtner, *The Temple and the Community in Qumran and the New Testament: A Comparative Study in the Temple Symbolism of the Qumran Texts and the New Testament*, SNTSMS 1 (Cambridge: Cambridge University Press, 1965).

role of the Temple cult.[24]   Although a direct dependency upon Leviticus cannot be sustained (nor should it be seriously postulated),[25] the conceptual background of 2:4-10 is best illustrated, and therefore illuminated, by the Levitical instructions of the Pentateuch.[26]   Consequently, both metaphor sections of this passage highlight the theme of divine election.   Given the above evidence, Martin's designation of the controlling metaphor of this cluster as "the elect household of God," should be shortened to "the elect of God."   Although "election" serves as

---

[24]The indication of the Temple being spiritualized may indicate that the date of 1 Peter is post-70, given the tendency within Christianity and Judaism to spiritualize the Temple after its destruction. Other examples of this tendency include John 2, *2 Clement* 9:2, *Epistle Barnabas* 4:11, *Ignat. Eph.* 9:1, *Ignat. Magn.* 7:2, *Ignat. Philad.* 7:2, *Gospel of Philip* 69,14-70,4, and *A Valentinian Exposition* 25,30-26,22. Not all post-70 Jews and Christians agreed with the movement away from the Temple cult to a spiritualized Temple/priesthood conception. For example, R. Eliezer held to a pro-priestly position (see Ben Zion Bokser's brief discussion of R. Eliezer's clash with other Jewish leaders over this issue, in Ben Zion Bokser, *Pharisaic Judaism in Transition: R. Eliezer the Great and Jewish Reconstruction After the War with Rome* [New York, NY: Bloch Publishing Company, 1935], esp. 75-83). A further example of a pro-Temple position in the post-70 period may be the Copper Scroll. If Manfred R. Lehmann ("The Key to Understanding the Copper Scroll: Where the Temple Tax Was Buried," *BAR* 19 [1993]: 38-43; "The Identification of the Copper Scroll Based on Its Technical Terms," *RevQ* 17 [1964]: 97-105) is correct, then this unique document recorded Jewish taxes collected (and hidden) between 70 and 90 C.E. in the hope of rebuilding the Temple. It is also important, however, to remember that spiritualization of the Temple cult was not limited to post-70 movements. The Qumran documents have furnished evidence that the Qumran community understood itself as a spiritual temple (see Gärtner *The Temple and the Community in Qumran and in the New Testament*). Allan J. McNicol ("The Eschatological Temple in the Qumran Pesher 4QFlorilegium 1:1-7," *Ohio Journal of Religious Studies* 5 [1977]: 133-41) has argued that 4QFlorilegium should be understood as viewing the temple as "a literal eschatological temple in the Future" (133), rather than a spiritualized community metaphor. Given the spiritualization of the Temple in Qumran in general, however, it is plausible that 1 Peter's spiritualization may not be as out of place within pre-70 Christianity as is typically assumed. The spiritualization tendency, furthermore, typified Diaspora Judaism, as McKelvey (*The New Temple: The Church in the New Testament,* 44; see also 125-33, where he specifically deals with 1 Peter) has noted. Therefore, it is possible that 1 Peter, as early Christian "diaspora" literature, could have also followed this tendency (see also Frances Y. Young, "Temple, Cult, and Law in Early Christianity," *NTS* 19 [1972/73]: 325; and Elisabeth Schüssler Fiorenza, "Cultic Language in Qumran and in the NT," *CBQ* 38 [1976]: 159-77).

[25]The possibility of a Levitical or "neo-Levitical" concept underlying 2:4-10 has been vehemently refuted by Elliott (*The Elect and the Holy*, Supplements to Novum Testamentum 12 [Leiden: E. J. Brill, 1966], 219-26).

[26]According to Origen (*Homily on Leviticus* 9,9,3 [trans. in Origen, *Homilies on Leviticus 1-16*, in *The Fathers of the Church* 83, trans. Gary Wayne Barkley (Washington, D.C.: The Catholic University of America Press, 1990), 196]) Peter (1 Peter 2:9) refers to Christians as priests, analogous to the Levitical priesthood. Thus, it may be possible to see a traditional understanding of 2:4-10 as imagery from Leviticus.

the fundamental sense of this cluster, the dual presence of οἶκος serves the function of articulating this generating metaphor so as to present the cluster as a topological unity.[27] All of these metaphorical elements are intimately correlative with the diaspora mentality of early Jewish and Christian communities. The compositional breakdown of the first metaphor cluster can now be outlined as follows:

ELECT PEOPLE OF GOD

‖

╓-------------------------------------╖

οἶκος-**NEWBIRTH (1:14-2:3)**   οἶκος-**TEMPLE/STONES (2:4-10)**

This exploration illustrates well the significance of a study of the compositional transitions in 1 Peter and their functional contribution to understanding the letter as a whole.

---

[27]See David G. Bradley, "The Origins of the Hortatory Material in the Letters of Paul" (Ph.D. dissertation, Yale University, 1947) for an extensive discussion of topos. Specifically note the unifying attribute of topological discourse: "The distinctive characteristic of the *topos* is that it is composed of more than one sentence dealing with the same subject. Often the *topos* has real literary unity and is a free moving discourse on a theme. Sometimes a *topos* may consist of an aggregation of proverbs or other short teachings which are on the same general subject. In this case the grouping of proverbs usually finds unity in the common subject matter" (40). The fact that key terms are used as linkages for the discussion has also been noted by Bradley: "In each of these cases, the key word serves a dual role; it is the name of the subject under discussion, and at the same time acts, by sight or sound, to link together the teaching which compose the *topos*" (39-40). Within the second section itself, οἶκος serves as the connective element for the subsections 2:4-5a (building metaphor) and 2:5b-10 (priestly metaphor) -- so observed by John Howard Bertram Masterman, *First Epistles of S. Peter* (London: Macmillan and Co., 1900), 96-97.

APPENDIX 2:

COMPOSITIONAL OUTLINE OF 1 PETER

Beyond the compositional adjustment to the break at 1 Peter 2:3 and 2:4 (see Appendix 1), other areas of adjustment have been made, such as the further breakdown of 2:4-10 into three subunits. The changes in 2:4-10 are based upon the shift in Temple/Priestly metaphors. The tripartite breakdown of the blessing assists in articulating the rhetorical flow of the passage, as the Petrine author shifts from epideictic praise to soteriological discourse to eschatological climax. The adjustment at 2:16-17 and 3:8-9 better indicates the introductory and closing function of these two units for the second metaphor cluster. The scriptural climax of 3:10-12, which serves along with 3:8-9 as the conclusion of the cluster, functions as a rhetorical climax which, consequently, sets the stage for the third metaphor cluster. The changes made in 3:13-4:1 explicate the exegetical work of Appendix 3, where the rhetorical strategy of the passage is best outlined. The adjustment at 5:6-11 is meant to articulate better the cosmic conflict in which Christ's victory over the Devil reflects the eschatological victory that the Petrine community and all Christians (5:9b) will share with Christ. One might also note that the third cluster begins with a typological discussion of Christ's victory, 3:13-4:1, and then ends with a cosmic victory of the community, 5:6-11. This parallel clearly sets forth a thematic inclusio for the third cluster on the issue of suffering and glory. This cosmic conflict in 5:6-11, and its victorious outcome, is meant to parallel dualistically the community conflict and, subsequently, the victory of the community over the opposition facing the addressees. Thus, an apocalyptic-eschatological mixture of paraenesis and consolation (an assurance of victory/glory) is used to bring the letter to a grand finale. The positive emphasis of 5:6-11 is emphatically summarized in a praiseful doxology (cf. 1:3-5). All changes to Martin's compositional outline have been presented in bold print.[1]

1. The Prescript (1:1-2)

2. The Blessing (1:3-12)

> **2.2. The Call to Worship (1:3-5)**
> **2.3. The Soteriological Reason for Praise (1:6-9)**
> **2.4. The Eschatological Climax (1:10-12)**

3. The Letter-body (1:13-5:12)

> 3.1. The Body-opening (1:13)
>
> 3.2. The Body-middle (1:14-5:11)
>
> > 3.2.1 **The First Cluster; Elect Status of the Community** (1:14-2:10)
> >
> > > 3.2.1.1 Οἶκος -- **New Birth Metaphors (1:14-2:3)**
> > > 3.2.1.1.1. Metaphor-obedient children: Be Holy (1:14-16)
> > > 3.2.1.1.2. Metaphor-children under a new *pater potestas*: Be reverent (1:17-21)
> > > 3.2.1.1.3. Metaphor-children in a new brotherhood: Love one another (1:22-25)
> > > **3.2.1.1.4. Metaphor-new born babes (2:1-3)**
> > >
> > > 3.2.1.2. Οἶκος -- **Temple/Priestly Metaphors (2:4-10)**
> > > **3.2.1.2.1. Metaphor-Living Stones: Being Built Into the Temple of God (2:4-5)**
> > > **3.2.1.2.2. Metaphor-Christ as Cornerstone (2:6-8)**

---

[1]Martin, *Metaphor and Composition in 1 Peter*, 271-73, offers his outline of 1 Peter, and it is used here with permission.

APPENDIX 3:
THE RHETORICAL STRATEGY OF 1 PETER 3:12-4:1

The author shifts into the third metaphor cluster with a concluding scriptural quotation.[1] The second metaphor cluster focuses upon the relationship of the Petrine community within their larger social world. The paraenetic discourse on how to live as "resident aliens" within their earthly "diaspora" is accomplished primarily through the Petrine household/station codes. The demarcation between insiders and outsiders is a key point: the Christian is an outsider in this world (2:11) due to being an insider in God's world (2:10). A cosmological dualism does not seem to be the key device in articulating this insider-outsider status. Rather a social/spiritual dualism seems to be the conceptual framework of this second cluster. The third cluster builds upon the second by looking at the suffering of Christians, specifically in relation to God's grace and righteous suffering.

The relationship between 3:12 and 3:13 is close. The transitional motion from the second metaphor cluster into the third is intimately related to the rhetorical strategy of the author. There are two connective elements that grammatically interconnect the two clusters here at the transitional juncture.

Syntactically, verses 12 and 13 are connected with the usage of κακά (v. 12) and κακώσων (v. 13). Several commentators have identified these as connective elements for the two verses. Ernest Best, for example, clearly recognizes the transitional role played by the verbal form in verse 13. The rhetorical question posed in verse 13 is a natural development from the preceding

---

[1]For a thorough exegesis of 1 Peter 3:9-12, and of the Petrine author's redactional activity, see Piper, "Hope as the Motivation of Love: 1 Peter 3:9-12," 212-31. For a discussion of the Petrine author's hermeneutical use of Psalm 34:13-17 (33:13-17 LXX), see Glenny, "The Hermeneutics of the Use of the Old Testament in 1 Peter," 129-53.

section into the persecution discussion of the new section.[2] Consequently, "harm" or "evil" (i.e. persecution) is a connective theme here in the transitional motion.[3] Thus, it is logical to conclude that the third metaphor cluster is intimately connected to the thematic flow of the letter. Out of the discussion of being temporary visitors in the world, the theme of suffering is developed. The outsider condition, already articulated, results in social exclusion from the insider status of the non-Christian.

The καί, which opens 3:13 and, thus, the third cluster, enhances the grammatical connection with verse 12. It is used as a connective particle of speech, in which a sequential development from the scriptural quotation in verse 12 is established. As J. N. D. Kelly put it, the syntactical relationship between κακά and κακώσων is confirmed with this introductory καί. Thus, "the rendering **then** is much to be preferred to 'And' (RV), 'Now' (RSV), or 'Beside' (E. G. Selwyn), for what we have is a fine example of the (primarily Semitic) use of the particle to preface an apodosis, with or without the protasis expressed, with the sense 'under the circumstances just set forth', or 'in the light of what has been said.'"[4] Unlike John 9:1, where the conjunctive particle is used to introduce a new narrative section separate from John 8, the particle used in 1 Peter 3:13 establishes a developmental connection between the second and third metaphor clusters. This is typical of the Petrine style, over against the Johannine style. As Beare succinctly put it: "The particle takes up the last phrase of the Scripture passage

---

[2] Best, *1 Peter*, 131. Cf. Cranfield, *The First Epistle of Peter*, 80-81.

[3] Beare (*The First Epistle of Peter*, 163) reads too much into 3:14 when he argues that "the thought of 'harm' is capable of being understood in a deeper sense." This "deeper sense," according to Beare, relates to "the inner life, attacking the integrity of the personality."

[4] J. N. D. Kelly, *A Commentary of the Epistles of Peter and Jude*, 139-40. See also Michaels, *1 Peter*, 185, who prefers a "then" or "and so" translation for καί. Furthermore, in 1 Peter the particle has been identified by most, if not all, commentators as a connective element between the two verses - - i.e. the particle indicates that the forthcoming discussion is based upon the previous material: Schutter, *Hermeneutic and Composition in 1 Peter*, 146-47; Goppelt, *A Commentary on 1 Peter*; Davids, *The First Epistle of Peter*, 129. This consecutive or conjunctive function of the particle in 3:13 is supported by the semantic connection already identified above on κακά (v. 12) and κακώσων (v. 13).

-- ποιοῦντας κακά -- and makes it the point of departure for a new line of thought."[5] Thus, in 1 Peter the compositional movement into the third cluster is accomplished with the use of a non-definite break.

This fluid movement, which is jointly accomplished with both the conjunctive καί and the syntactical relationship between κακά and κακώσων, is closely related to the rhetorical intention, and stylistic formulation, of 3:13-4:1, as well as the cluster as a whole. It is to this rhetorical approach that we now turn our attention.

The transition from 1 Peter 3:12 to 3:13 is closely related to the rhetorical strategy of the Petrine author. The author opens the third metaphor cluster with the question, "Now who will harm you if you are eager to do what is good?" The question is grammatically interconnected with the scriptural quotation preceding it.

The rhetorical function of this question, and its relationship with 3:10-12, can be discovered by analyzing Quintilian's discussion of "questions" and "bases" (*Oratoria* 3.5-3.6). Quintilian identifies two types of questions.[6] The "*indefinite* questions are those which may be maintained or impugned without reference to persons, time or place and the like" (3.5.5). There is, in essence, an abstract quality to indefinite questions, which thereby make them applicable to various situations. An example, which Quintilian provides, would be "is the world governed by providence?" (3.5.6). Other terms for this first type of question are theses, propositions, causes, general questions relating to civil life, and questions suited for philosophical discussion (3.5.5-6). The second type of questions presented by Quintilian are called "*definite* questions [which] involve facts, persons, time and the like" (3.5.7). Definite questions are more specific than indefinite questions, and are therefore related to particular situations that are of specific concern. An example, as supplied by Quintilian, would be "should Cato

---

[5]Beare, *The First Epistle of Peter*, 162.

[6]See Smyth, *Greek Grammar*, § 2636ff, where he discusses "interrogative sentences (questions)."

marry?" (3.5.8). In contrast, an indirect question would run, "should a man marry?" The latter is abstract and general, while the former is specific. Other designations for this second type of question are special questions, hypotheses, and causes (3.5.7-9). Behind each direct question stands an indirect question, even if only by implication (3.5.9-10).

Quintilian's discussion quickly moves into an extensive discussion of *bases* (3.5.17-3.6.104, and then developed further in 3.7). For the sake of this present study of 1 Peter 3:12-13, a brief summary of Quintilian's discussion of *stasis* theory will suffice. It is important, however, to remember that Quintilian is primarily concerned with the forensic usage of questions and *bases*, such as in a courtroom, and, therefore, should only be used in a general sense when applied to non-forensic settings such as our present letter.

Bases function as the propositions on which the case in question hinges. All the questions raised in relation to the case must relate back to this foundational premise, as the *basis* serves as the point at which the case needs to be settled. It is true that certain questions do not have a *basis* proper, for the reasons behind the statement/accusation must be presented in order to establish the proposition and thus the *basis* (3.6.76). Every *basis* "originates from the question" (3.6.72), and therefore questions can be used to locate their specific *basis*. Quintilian offers several examples of how a *basis* can be determined, one of which includes:

> "Horatius has committed a crime, for he has killed his sister." "He has not committed a crime, since it was his duty to kill her for mourning the death of an enemy." The question is whether this was a justifiable reason, and the *basis* is one of *quality* (3.6.76).

In this example, the accusation has been raised with regard to the murder of Horatius' sister. The question arises from the rationale for Horatius' action: "was this a justifiable reason?" This serves as the premise upon which the case will ensue.

In 1 Peter 3:13 the Petrine author raises a question, "who will harm you?" The question, however, has a propositional premise that follows in 3:13b: "if you are eager to do what is good?" From this question, it could be determined that the *basis* of the discussion is to determine whether or not the Petrine community is truly being "τοῦ ἀγαθοῦ ζηλωταὶ γένησθε" or not.[7] If this were the case, then the third part of the letter-body would prove that the Petrine Christians are not being "eager to do what is good," as they are under a state of suffering and persecution. If this were the case, then the letter should be interpreted as a reprimand, rather than an encouraging exhortation. The third metaphor cluster, however, is not intended to reprimand the Petrine community, for the propositional rationale for 3:13a is further supplemented by the preceding scriptural quotation.

First Peter 3:12 ends the second metaphor cluster by stating that "the eyes of the Lord are on the righteous . . . but the face of the Lord is against those who do evil." The καί and the ἐάν in 3:13 establish that both 3:12 and 3:13b function as the qualifiers for 3:13a: The Lord is for those who are righteous and against those who do evil, and therefore the Lord is taking care of the Petrine community who are righteous and is opposed to those who would potentially do harm to these

---

[7] I do not wish to enter into a debate as to whether or not this phrase should be translated as "zealous for the good" with Jewish or Greek interpretive connotations. Martin, in an appendix, has argued that the diaspora metaphor helps to determine that τοῦ ἀγαθοῦ should be seen "as a euphemism for the name *God*" (*Metaphor and Composition in 1 Peter*, 288). There are two problems, however, with this whole debate, including Martin's position. First, the social make-up of the Petrine community, as well as the Petrine author, has yet to be established well enough to evaluate any such position. Second, an artificial demarcation between "Jewish" and "Greek" aspects of Christianity is presupposed. As scholarship is continually, and convincingly, articulating, the interactive dynamics of the Greco-Roman world make it extremely difficult to determine exactly what is "Christian," "Jewish" ("Diaspora" and "Palestinian" Jewish), and "Greek." For example, Robert G. Hall ("Isaiah's Ascent to See the Beloved: An Ancient Jewish Source for the *Ascension of Isaiah*," *JBL* 113 [1994]: 463-84) has strongly argued that the demarcation between Christian, Jewish, and Gnostic elements in antiquity is methodologically flawed. Hall concludes: ". . . it seems best to think of the Vision of Isaiah as a unity. In the meantime, the Vision of Isaiah is sufficiently Jewish to illustrate the history of Judaism, sufficiently Christian to illustrate the history of Christianity, and sufficiently gnostic to illustrate the history of gnosticism" (484). I believe that the same could be said of 1 Peter in relation to Jewish and Greek influences. In essence, first and second century Christianity sufficiently interacted with various philosophical and religious systems during its initial development to make it multidimensional in nature. The dynamics of the Mediterranean region, as I have argued elsewhere, encouraged such a multi-dimensional development (Tite, "Pax, Peace and the New Testament," 319-22).

Christians.[8] Indeed, the theme of a protective almighty deity is once again raised here at this compositional transition, as it was at 2:9![9] Here, however, the intensity of the danger, "harm" rather than "alien status," and of the protection, passively being in the protective care of God to God actively opposing the enemies of the elect community, is much higher than in 2:9-11.

Consequently, the premise upon which the question is both raised and thus answered is one of God's protective care for his loyal people. From this emerges the ideal general question, in 3:13: "Now who will harm you if you are eager to do what is good?" This is a general question (or "indirect question"), which has an unspoken/implied ideal answer of "no one can harm us" -- based on verse 12, the ideal basis, where God is for the righteous (those "zealous for the good") and against the evil ones (those who would cause "harm").[10] From this ideal situation (premise) the Petrine author makes a declaration of God's goodness that rivals the opening "Εὐλογητὸς ὁ θεὸς καὶ πατὴρ τοῦ κυρίου ἡμῶν Ἰησοῦ Χριστοῦ" of

---

[8]For a broader discussion of this theme, see Martin, *Metaphor and Composition in 1 Peter*, 210-15; and Everett Ferguson, "Spiritual Sacrifices in Early Christianity and its Environment," *ANRW* 23.2 (1980): 1151-89.

[9]It is my hypothesis that 2:9-10 contains a "protective" theme along with the elect status of the Petrine community. This is present in 2:9-10 on the basis of the phrase λαὸς εἰς περιποίησιν (2:9), which I translate as "a people preserved unto God" rather than the usual "a people for God's own possession." I argue this interpretation on the basis of an etymological analysis of "περιποίησιν," a source-contextual study of the LXX passages from which the scriptural allusions of 2:9 may be drawn, and the contextual basis of 1 Peter. This is further substantiated by the community's reception of "mercy" in 2:10, which is contingent upon their being the elect people of God. First Peter 2:10 accomplishes this heightened presentation through the rhetorical devices of reduplication and synonmous/antithetical parallelism within a nicely balanced prose -- the two primary clauses and the two subordinant clauses. The proctective thrust of λαὸς εἰς περιποίησιν has not be widely recognized among commentators. John Rogers is one notable exception. Writing in 1650, Rogers comments that "this is a comfort that God makes such special reckoning of his; therefore though we have many and mighty Enemies, yet we need not fear: God is on our side, he is about us, as the Mountains about *Jerusalem*; they must dig down God ere they can come at his, overcome God ere they can conquer his" (*A Godly & Fruitful Exposition Upon all the First Epistle of Peter*, 272).

[10]Such a concept can be found elsewhere in the ancient literature. See, for example, Matthew 10:28; Luke 21:16-18; and Plato, *Apology* 41d. In these examples, the idea raised is that those who face opposition, due to their virtuous life-style, will not be harmed. For the Petrine community this is important, as it reflects the way in which they had evidently reacted in regard to the struggles that they faced due to being Christians.

the blessing-section (1:3). This is a high point in the letter, and may well have served as a climactic conclusion to the second metaphor cluster had the author wished to end with such an eschatological division of the protected "insiders" and the opposed "outsiders." Indeed, the discussion could end here with the ideal *basis*, ideal "indirect" question, and the implied ideal answer, had this letter been merely a theoretical, or abstract theological, discussion. Yet, the community situation (or perceived situation) is not merely one of theoretical concern, so the discussion continues with "ἀλλ' εἰ καὶ πάσχοιτε διὰ δικαιοσύνην . . ." (3:14).[11]

The actual community situation facing the recipients does not correlate to the ideal *basis*. For the Petrine community, it would seem that the ideal *basis* does not reflect their experience of community suffering. Thus, there is an unspoken situational *basis*. The situational *basis* is the suffering, or persecution, felt/perceived by the Petrine community. The situation of the community has arisen due to their being Christians. Although the situation of the community is unspoken, through the rhetorical strategy of suppression, it is clearly known to both the Petrine author and the Petrine community. It is important to remember that a letter is one side of a conversation, and therefore the author of 1 Peter would have had to anticipate the response of his/her audience. The situational *basis* is the unspoken crisis with which the author must contend, for this is the *basis* upon which the audience would respond and critique the author's theoretical deliberation.

From this *basis* arises the specific, or "direct," question in response to the author's ideal *basis* and ideal indirect question. Note that Quintilian observes that the direct question arises from the indirect question (3.5.8). In 1 Peter 3:12-13,

---

[11]Bennett (*The General Epistles*, 229-30) recognized the need that the Petrine author felt to continue the discussion: "The conclusion seems obvious and necessary, that no one can harm them; but nevertheless seems also quite at variance with experience." Similarly, Benson (*A Paraphrase*, 246) identifies the same situational concern, but in regard to verse 12. Benson (*A Paraphrase*, 250) also recognizes that 3:14 was necessary, as the recipients would have objected to the idealistic claim of verse 13, and therefore the Petrine author answered any objections in anticipation.

the situational direct question (which, like the situational *basis*, is implied and not stated in the text) emerges as a response to the ideal indirect question (and its implied ideal answer). First Peter 3:14 indicates the situational question (and thus the situational *basis*) when the author attempts to counter the opposition to his/her ideal basis-question-answer that would arise from the situational *basis*-question. The situational *basis* is one of suffering, or harm, being done to the community. From this *basis* naturally emerges the situational direct question, "but we, who are 'zealous for the good,' are indeed suffering/being harmed, so why is God allowing this to happen if he is indeed for the righteous?" The situational question brings into question the validity of the Christian faith by raising the issue of theodicy concerning why God allows suffering, specifically our suffering. This situation in the community further raises the danger of defection from the faith within the Petrine community. To this the author of 1 Peter must answer anticipatively.[12]

F. W. Beare is one of the commentators to recognize the difficulty of this passage, i.e., how to deal with the issue of the righteous suffering. Yet, he does not recognize the underlying rhetorical strategy. Instead, Beare merely understands the Petrine author as advocating a naive position of overcoming potential suffering through zealous goodness, thereby underestimating the author's

---

[12]The presence of a rhetorical question and implied answer along this "ideal" train of thought has already been observed by Davids (*The First Epistle of Peter*, 129): "The rhetorical question asks, 'Who will do you harm?' The implied answer is, 'No one.' But this answer causes commentators problems, for Peter in the very next verse brings in the concept of suffering for righteousness." After outlining some options for understanding this passage (129-30), Davids states (130): "While none, even under their own pagan codes of proper conduct, will have grounds for harming Christians, some Christians will suffer. Our verse, then, is a transition from the idea of minimizing suffering through virtue to a renewed teaching of how to behave when one suffers anyway." Davids (130) accepts Goppelt's "proverbial" reading. The rhetorical strategy explored in our present study better explains the seemly paradoxical flow in 3:13a and 3:13b -- i.e. they are not separate, but rhetorically connected in the author's epistolary dialogue and his consolatory-paraenetical objectives. Smyth (*Greek Grammar*, §2640) states that rhetorical questions "are questions asked for effect and not for information, since the speaker knows the answer in advance and either does not wait for, or himself gives, the answer," and, furthermore, "rhetorical questions awaken attention and express various shades of emotion; and are often used in passing to a new subject." Thus, in 1 Peter the rhetorical question at 3:13 indicates a transitional motion in the text; one which has a rhetorical function in regard to *ethos*.

skill as a rhetorician.[13] The Petrine author has designed a rhetorically complex presentation in 3:12-4:1 in order to encourage a "community in crisis." The author is not an unskilled writer, nor is he merely advocating a simplistic and naive position. He realizes that the difficulties facing the community are serious and threaten their faith at the very core.[14]

The opening verses of the third cluster function as an introductory statement of the paraenesis of this cluster. From verses 18-22 the author enters a typological discussion to answer the situational question, with its potentially devastating consequences. The passage is primarily a christological typology of Christ's suffering as it led to glory/victory.[15] Through the process of suffering, Christ attained his exaltation. According to Shimada, the presence of a descent (humiliation)/ascent (glorification) theme is absolutely clear.[16] This is a correct observation.[17] The passage moves from the suffering of Christ (3:18-19) to a

---

[13]Beare, *The First Epistle of Peter*, 162. Beare also sees the optative mood as indicating "a future possibility which is far from vivid" and therefore "no other part of the Discourse reflects so clearly the fact that it was composed before the storm of persecution had broken. The time when men would be condemned to torture and death simply 'as Christians' (4:16) had not yet come" (163).

[14]Cf. Bennett, *The General Epistles*, 230, who states the situation as follows: "Peter himself is much more anxious lest that should be a failure of Christian conduct."

[15]The typological nature of this passage, as well as 2 Peter 2:4-9, has been aptly outlined by Jean Daniélou (*From Shadows to Reality: Studies in Biblical Typology of the Fathers*, trans. Dom Wulstan Hibberd [London: Burns & Oates, 1960]). The typology of Noah and the Flood follows the central themes of "a catastrophe which will annihilate the sinful world, a remnant of which will be saved. Such was the mystery accomplished in the time of Noah, which the author [of the Book of Enoch] relates to prefiguring times to come" (75). This theme is carried over into Christian typology, with christology and baptism playing key roles in presenting this "remnant" eschatological theme as a present reality within the life of the Christian. Within this typological presentation, the *Christus Victor* theme becomes paramount. Within the rhetorical strategy of 1 Peter, we can see how this Flood typology fits in well with both the diaspora metaphor ("remnant" theme) and the eschatological victory theme that pervades the letter.

[16]Shimada, "The Formulary Material," 318.

[17]The presence of a christological creedal formula in this passage, like any source hypotheses in 1 Peter, is questionable -- though not necessarily impossible (Shimada, "The Formulary Material," 316-18). Shimada further perceives 3:20-21 as a redactional insertion into this creedal formula. A hymnic source is not, however, seen as an acceptable option for Shimada.

divergence into the "proclamation to the spirits in prison" (3:19-20) and a Noachic typological portrayal of baptism (3:21a).[18] The passage then shifts into an "upward" (ascent) motion in 3:21b, with "the resurrection of Jesus Christ" and then climaxing with Christ having "gone into heaven and is at the right hand of God, with angels, authorities, and powers made subject to him" (3:22). Christ is clearly presented as the one who attained glory and honour through the process of suffering. The suffering of Christ is not the focal point of Petrine christology, but rather it is his glorification.[19] The Noachic typology of 3:20 also functions to exemplify this suffering/glorification theme. Although Feinberg has correctly stated that this Flood type needs to be understood within the literary context of the passage, rather than as a break in the text, he has incorrectly read the type far too literally in asserting the theory of Christ preaching through Noah in the antediluvian period.[20] When seen in the context of the rhetorical question of 3:13,

---

[18]Although 3:18-22 can be described as a "digression," Beare's contention should not be accepted. Beare (*The First Epistle of Peter*, 170) understands this passage as "in some degree a digression, moving away from the subject immediately in hand," as the Petrine author attempts to "relate Christian doctrine of suffering to the saving experience of baptism" -- as based on Romans 6. Beare sees 1 Peter's author as being unable fully to grasp and apply Pauline thought in this passage. First Peter does *not* move away from the "subject immediately in hand," but, as will be shown below, develops the main idea of this passage through a typological discourse on the glorification/victory of Christ. Furthermore, it is unnecessary to view the author as less intellectually gifted than Paul. The Petrine author is obviously distinct in his thought, yet this does not make him inferior to Paul. Also, there is no reason to believe that the Petrine author is dependent upon Pauline thought, let alone Romans, for this passage (even though 1 Peter 4:1 and Romans 6:7 may both be individual variants of a proverbial saying).

[19]For a similar appraisal of Petrine christology, as being intertwined with the eschatological suffering/glorification of Christ, see Earl Richard, "The Functional Christology of First Peter" (in *Perspectives on First Peter*, 121-39, specifically 133-39). Also, see Pearson, "The Christological Hymnic Pattern of 1 Peter," 182-245, where she argues for the presence of the suffering/glories schema (following Schutter), with Isaiah 53-54 as the conceptual source for 1 Peter 3:18-22. Furthermore, Pearson recognized the role of theodicy in this passage.

[20]John S. Feinberg, "1 Peter 3:18-20, Ancient Mythology, and the Intermediate State," *WTJ* 48 (1986): 303-36. Furthermore, I have no difficulty in accepting Dalton's (*Christ's Proclamation to the Spirits*) theory that Christ's proclamation was to evil powers (that he was victorious over) upon his ascension. Dalton's hypothesis not only fits into the socioreligious context of early Christianity, but also amplifies the victory motif of this passage. Cf. Dalton, "1 Peter 3:19 Reconsidered" (*The New Testament Age: Essays in Honor of Bo Reicke*, vol. 1, ed. William C. Weinrich [Macon, GA: Mercer University Press, 1984], 95-105).

the Noah exemplar can best be seen as an example of the christological exemplar. That is, the Noachic type functions to amplify the theme of victory through suffering. Indeed, the Flood tale serves exceptionally well in this regard. The suffering of Christ, therefore, was merely the vehicle by which this glory was achieved. The entire discourse of 3:13-21 is both christological and soteriological in presentation.

The presence of the optative mood in 3:14 is used to downplay the seriousness of the community's suffering, in contrast with their eschatological glory. That is, the optative designates the suffering as being remote. The author does not wish to say that suffering has not, is not, and will not occur (the situational premise clearly nullifies such an interpretation of the optative),[21] but rather that in relation to their "glory," the "harm" facing the Christian community is not the focal point. This is further supported by the καὶ τίς construction at the opening of 3:13. Καί, followed by the interrogative τίς, places additional stress to the interrogative.[22] Consequently, 3:13a could be translated emphatically as follows: "*WHO* could *POSSIBLY* harm you, if you are zealous for what is right?" As Smyth has noted, καί "*before* an interrogative expression marks an objection

---

[21]Best, *1 Peter*, 132, says that "in a conditional clause, as here, it [the optative mood] implies that there is no certainty of fulfillment of the condition, but it goes too far to speak of it as an unlikely contingency; it may or may not happen." Best, quoting M. Zerwick (*Biblical Greek*, trans. J. Smith [Rome: Scripta Pontifici Instituti Biblici, 1963], 111), says "St. Peter well knows that in fact such sufferings are eminently probable in the Christian life, and indeed perhaps already a reality for his readers. His tact, however, leads him, when speaking of sufferings to those who are seeking to avoid them, to put the matter on the theoretical plane."

[22]For a discussion of interpreting the stress in the καὶ τίς construction, see J. D. Denniston, *The Greek Particles* (2nd ed. [Oxford: The Clarendon Press, 1959], 312-13). If the interrogative had preceded the particle (with the optative in this clause), then a stronger emphasis would have emerged in 3:13, with "the very possibility of something is denied, so that further discussion of it is seen to be unnecessary" (314). Although the Petrine author could have used a "τίς καί" construction to denote this to his recipients, he seems to have preferred the less emphatic "καὶ τίς" construction -- probably so as to set the stage for the typological discussion offered following the rhetorical question (a discussion that may have been ruled out as technically unnecessary with the more emphatic presentation). In other words, the author is rhetorically sensitive even within his grammatical constructions, such as with the indirect question of 3:13.

occasioned by surprise or indignation."[23]   The Petrine author opens the third cluster so as to generate a mood of indignation. This indignation shifts the focus of the Christians away from the negative aspects of their diaspora status, thereby negating the suffering premise for defection. Consequently, the optative mood is best understood within the context of this passage's rhetorical strategy.

The opening of 4:1 (οὖν -- "therefore") indicates that the christological typology is meant as a example for imitation.[24] As Monnier commented; "οὖν rattache ce qui va être dit à l'oeuvre du Christ souffrant (3, 18) et en tire les conséquences morales."[25] The *imatio Christi* theme of 3:13-4:1 is further indicated earlier in the passage. The shift into the christological discourse at 3:18 is preceded by a discussion of the suffering of the Petrine community. The ὅτι καὶ of 3:18 clearly links the exhortations of 3:14-17 with 3:18-22. Indeed, the exemplary nature of 3:18-22 is further indicated by "For it is better to suffer for doing good, if suffering should be God's will, than to suffer for doing evil" (3:17) immediately prior to ὅτι καὶ. Thus, the Christ typology is an example of "suffering for doing good."[26]   Furthermore, the shift toward the Petrine community's soteriological roots in 3:21 adds to the typological nature of Christ as an/the exemplar for the community (". . . baptism . . . now saves you" and "for a good conscience, through [διά] the resurrection of Jesus Christ"). Drawing upon J. R. Lumby, Davids notes that Christ's suffering exemplifies the following: "First, it is unjust suffering." "Second, the Suffering of Christ was 'righteous on

---

[23]Smyth, *Greek Grammar*, §2872.

[24]To recognize an *imatio Christi* theme in this passage is not a new idea, but was seen even by The Venerable Bede (*Commentary on the Seven Catholic Epistles*, 101, 107), and by Benson (*A Paraphrase*, 264).

[25]Monnier, *La Première*, 190.

[26]Glasgow (*The General Epistles*, 71) sees that "this entire section [3:13-4:11], the first division which we study here, centres around Christian character, which is Christ-likeness or Christ in us. The balancing thoughts back and forth in this section are suffering and glory." The exemplary nature of 3:18-22 is, furthermore, well observed by Monnier, *La Première*, 167.

behalf of the unrighteous.'" "Third, the purpose of the suffering of Christ was 'to lead you to God.'" "Fourth, the death of Christ did not destroy him, just as death will not destroy the Christian sufferer."[27] The strong interwoven nature of the christological exemplar of 3:18-22 and the exhortations of 3:14-17 and 4:1, clearly indicate that the hypothesis of an underlying hymn behind 3:18-22, such as postulated by Boismard, is not plausible. Although there is indeed a shift from the strict community exhortations at 3:18, and then only picked up again at 4:1, it needs to be understood that 3:18-22 is embedded into the paraenetical fabric of the passage. As Webb more accurately indicates, the Petrine author may indeed be using liturgical or hymnic material in the formation of 3:18-19,[28] yet the passage functions as substantiation for the argument of 3:13-17 and, thus, 3:13-4:6 "is best understood to be a logical unit whose primary purpose is to encourage the readers."[29] Thus, the potential presence of a source does not nullify either the compositional integrity of the text nor its thematic or rhetorical flow of thought. It has been established already that typology is a tool of moral exhortation.[30]

---

[27]Davids, *The First Epistle of Peter*, 134-36; J. R. Lumby, "1 Peter III. 17," *Expositor* 5 (1890): 142-43.

[28]Webb, "The Apocalyptic Perspective of First Peter," 54: "The literary form of this passage suggests the use of liturgical material. While this assumption is generally recognized, the identification and extent of the material is debated. W. J. Dalton argues persuasively for the balanced conclusion that 3:18,22 are from an early Christ-hymn and 3:19-21 are an interpolation by the author which incorporates extra-biblical tradition and catechetical material on baptism."

[29]Webb, "The Apocalyptic Perspective of First Peter," 76-77. Webb, however, holds that 3:13-17 serves two purposes; "1) to state the blessedness of suffering for righteousness (3:13-14a,17), and 2) to describe the righteous response to this suffering which is to maintain one's Christian identity (3:14-16)". Consequently, he sees the theme of theodicy in this passage (a theme connected to the sufferings/glories schema), even though he is correct in identifying the unity of this passage and the rhetorical function of 3:18-21. Indeed, he clearly recognizes that 3:18-21, which, he argues, is not a moral example, is "best understood as providing the theological grounds for 3:13-17" (75).

[30]Bradley, "The Origins of the Hortatory Material in the Letters of Paul," 52: "There was employed in Hellenistic literature a favorite device to make vivid and concrete the desirability of embodying in one's life the virtues recommended by a teacher or of showing specifically why certain vices should be shunned. This was done by means of a *typos*, the characterization of a virtue or vice as typified in the life of a well-known person." In 1 Peter this is done with the presentation of the glorification of Christ as an exemplar for the Petrine community. Thus, typological presentation, such as in 3:18-22, is a key tool of paraenesis -- specifically the paraenesis of 1 Peter.

Furthermore, as Best correctly observed, the thematic development of suffering in 3:18-22 is in alignment with that of 3:13-17.[31] Consequently, although Boismard is correct in identifying the passage as following "le style parénétique," with a christological emphasis,[32] he is incorrect in stating that 3:18-22 is a break in the paraenetic discussion, and thus evidence of a hymnic source.[33]

Thus, the Petrine community is also to go through suffering in order to attain "glory" or victory. Martin has thoroughly established that the crisis facing the Petrine community constituted, to a large degree, the question of "glory" (δόξα). Within the Greco-Roman world, one's value was determined by one's status within society. In discussing the meaning of δόξα, Martin summarizes as follows:

> Greco-Roman society was an hierarchical society. Esteem and reputation, not only by one's peers and superiors but also by one's inferiors, were highly sought after. Socialization involved performing one's duties, discharging one's responsibilities, and relating to others so one could attain δόξα. An extended discussion of Cicero regarding this subject demonstrates that attainment of δόξα was the objective of socialization and thus paraenesis in his society. (Cicero, *De Officiis* 2.9-11)[34]

---

[31]Best, *1 Peter*, 149: "Christ is introduced as example and, once introduced, controls the thought; we move from his atoning death to his resurrection and victory over the evil powers; this victory serves to assure his followers that there is nothing to harm them if they stand firm for what is right (3:13)."

[32]Boismard, *Quatre hymnes baptismales*, 57: "Bien des exégètes déjà ont admis que, pour illustrer par l'exemple du Christ son exhortation à la patience dans des persécutions, l'auteur de la *Prima Petri* avait cité plus ou moins littéralement un texte liturgique plus ancien. En effect, la section parénétique sur la conduite morale à tenir au milieu des païens (3, 13 et 4, 6) est interrompue par un développement Christologique dont les formules rythmées rappellent le style hymnique et non le style parénétique."

[33]Even Beare (*The First Epistle of Peter*, 177) rejects the separation of 3:18-22 and 4:6 from the literary context of 1 Peter. Beare claims that these verses are not "glosses" later inserted into the text, indicating that "not only is there no manuscript authority for rejecting them, but there is nothing in the style or diction to betray the hand of a glossator." At 4:1, however, the "ὅτι ὁ παθὼν σαρκὶ πέπαυται ἁμαρτίας" may indeed be (as Beare contends, 179) a proverbial saying, as a potential variant appears in Romans 6:7.

[34]Martin, *Metaphor and Composition in 1 Peter*, 108. This is followed by an extended quotation from Cicero, *De Officiis* 2.9-11, where Cicero outlined succinctly the significance of "glory" for Hellenistic socialization (108-10).

The rhetorical situation facing the Petrine community was one in which δόξα had not been attained through adhering to the precepts of the Christian lifestyle. The reverse had in fact occurred. Thus, the Petrine author is faced with a paradoxical situation, in which the venue to δόξα evidently had failed for the Christian community. The presentation of Jesus as an exemplar for the community is an attempt to justify their social status, by placing the community's "glory" into an eschatological frame of reference. This is clearly the rhetorical approach taken in 3:18-22. As Christ attained his δόξα through suffering and reproach, so also must the Petrine community attain their social status within an eschatological process of suffering.[35] In order to encourage the recipients to continue along the precepts of Christianity, the author presents a dualistic earthly vs. heavenly concept of "glory." As Martin aptly summarized, "in 1 Peter the recipients are urged to act or not act in certain ways so that they can attain not fleeting glory but eternal glory."[36] As F. L. Cross stated, in regard to 1 Peter 2:20, "Here we are given the religious basis of all suffering by the Christian, its direct relation to Christ as the archetypal Sufferer, the true Pasch."[37]

In regard to the situational question and the ideal *basis*-question-answer, this eschatological typology reaffirms the ideal question-answer within the

---

[35]Cf. Weiss, *A Commentary on the New Testament*, 287: "But if this is the case, then we, too, are to arm ourselves with the same motive which induced Him to suffer, namely with the thought of the blessed results of such sufferings."

[36]Martin, *Metaphor and Composition in 1 Peter*, 116.

[37]Cross, *1 Peter: A Paschal Liturgy*, 21. The concern over honour/shame within early Christian communities has been similarly observed in Hebrews by David A. DeSilva ("Despising Shame: A Cultural-Anthropological Investigation of the Epistle to the Hebrews," *JBL* 113 (1994): 438-61). A similiar presentation of the glory/shame theme can be found in such Gnostic texts as *Authoritative Teaching* 32, 9-16: "And she learns about her depth and runs into her fold, while her shepherd stands at the door. In return for all the shame and scorn, then, that she received in this world, she receives ten thousand times the grace and glory" (cited from George W. MacRae's translation in *The Nag Hammadi Library in English*, 3rd ed. rev., ed. James M. Robinson [San Francisco: HarperCollins, 1988], 309). The issue of the Christian's earthly or heavenly attainment of glory pervaded the early Christian movement, and, therefore, it is not surprising to find it arising so prominently in 1 Peter. See Elliott, "Disgraced Yet Graced. The Gospel according to 1 Peter in the Key of Honor and Shame," *BTB* 25 (1995): 166-78.

situational basis. The situational premise of the Petrine community is not to be understood as contradictory with the ideal premise offered in 3:10-12, but rather as evidence of the eschatological process that God has initiated for the Christians fully to attain their δόξα. Indeed, the "glory" that the Christian will achieve is greater than any form of social glorification that can be attained in this earthly realm. Consequently, the Petrine author has utilized the paraenetic tool of *typos* rhetorically to validate the ideal premise of 3:10-12, and thereby justify the Petrine community's confidence in God. As Johnston has correctly observed, this passage is practical in its orientation, as it addresses "a *persecuted* Church."[38] This is intended to dissuade the recipients from defecting from the Christian faith. From this rhetorical presentation, we can observe the careful concern that the Petrine author has in offering a consolatory thrust within his paraenetic discussion.

The transitional motion from the second metaphor cluster to the third is intimately interwoven with the rhetorical strategy of 1 Peter. The closing of the second metaphor cluster sets forth a positive climactic finale for the second cluster. Yet, in preparation for the third metaphor cluster, the author also utilizes the scriptural quotation in 3:10-12 to set up the rhetorical discussion that is used to initiate the third cluster's theme of suffering in the dispersion. The Petrine author has responded to the community situation in such a way as to render this passage a *stasis of definition*: he agrees that the Petrine Christians are in the midst of suffering, yet does not agree that this indicates that God is unjust or has breached his promise to them (3:12). Rather, the Petrine author redefines their suffering along an eschatological trajectory, where suffering is part of the process of attaining glory. Paraenetic techniques -- namely the christological and Noachic

---

[38]Johnston, *First Epistle of Peter*, 30. Johnston also recognizes the critical role that Christ plays in this practical address: "The fact, signally illustrated in the case of the Redeemer Himself, that suffering for righteousness' sake in flesh brings quickening in spirit, is fitted to give to His people under persecution peculiar consolation and peculiar stimulus (iii. 18 - iv. 6)." Johnston understands Petrine christology as moving beyond mere atonement theology to Christ's suffering being an *example* for Christians to follow and with which to be encouraged (38). He also recognizes the mediatorial role of Christ.

typologies, as well as the use of the optative mood[39] -- are used to represent this position. The concept of "righteous suffering," furthermore, is closely connected to the diaspora mentality, as is well illustrated in *Susanna*.[40] The two clusters, therefore, should be seen as being closely interwoven, as articulated through the transitional motion from 3:12 to 3:13.

---

[39]The four forms of *stasis* are: (1) *stasis of conjecture*, where the act is denied; (2) *stasis of definition*, where the act is admitted but redefined; (3) *stasis of quality*, where the act and definition are accepted, but is explained away for other reasons; and (4) *stasis of objection*, where the whole procedings are objected to on the basis of a technicality. Recently, Martin has offered an intriguing application of *stasis* theory to Galatians ("Apostasy to Paganism: The Rhetorical Stasis of the Galatian Controversy," *JBL* 114 [1995]: 437-61). The application of *stasis* theory to other Christian origin texts, such as I have attempted to a degree in regard to 1 Peter, may prove useful in better understanding the rhetorical argumentation of these ancient texts.

[40]*Susanna* (Daniel 13) relates a narrative of a woman who is wrongly accused of adultery by the two elders who have lusted after her. The setting is Babylon during the Exile. In *Sus.* 42-43, she declares not only her innocence, but also gives a plea to God for assistance. In 47 God "heard her cry." The source for the suffering she faced (which almost led to her death) would seem to be the lust of the two elders. Yet, the source for unjust suffering in this document is stated as closely related to the diaspora condition of the Jews (*Sus.* 5). The thrust of the text, in relation to the righteous sufferer, is that the diaspora is a hostile setting for the righteous, yet the sufferers should stand fast in their morality and loyalty to God, for the Lord will vindicate those who rely upon him during their time of exile. The theme of divine protective care in the midst of suffering is a key element.

BIBLIOGRAPHY

BOOKS AND COMMENTARIES

Ambroggi, Pietro De. *Le Epistole Cattoliche Di Giacomo. Pietro, Giovanni e Giuda.* La Sacra Biblia 14.1, Torino: Marietti, 1947.

Aretius Benedictus. *Commentarii in Domini nostri Jesu Christi Novum Testamentum.* Geneva: Petrum & Iacobum Chouet, 1607.

Augusti, J. C. W. *Die Katholischen Briefe.* Lemgo: Meyersche Buchhandlung, 1801.

Balch, David L. *Let Wives Be Submissive: The Domestic Code in 1 Peter.* SBLMS 26, Chico, CA.: Scholars Press, 1981.

Balz, Horst and Wolfgang Schrage. *Die Katholischen Briefe.* Das Neue Testament Deutsch 10. Göttingen: Vandenhoeck & Ruprecht, 1973.

Barnes, Albert. *Notes, Explanatory and Practical, on the General Epistles of James, Peter, John and Jude.* New York, NY: Harper & Brothers, 1848.

Bauer, Walter. *Die Katholischen Briefe des Neuen Testaments,* Religionsgeschichtliche Volksbücher für die deutsche christliche Gegenwart 1.20. Tübingen: J. C. B. Mohr (Paul Siebeck), 1910.

_____. *Orthodoxy and Heresy in Earliest Christianity.* Trans. Robert A. Kraft and Gerhard Krodel. Philadelphia, PA: Fortress Press, 1971 [1934].

Beare, Francis W. *The First Epistle of Peter.* Oxford: Basil Blackwell, 1958.

Beck, Johannes Tobias. *Erklärung der Briefe Petri.* Gütersloh: C. Bertelsmann, 1986.

Bede, The Venerable. *The Commentary on the Seven Catholic Epistles of Bede the Venerable.* Trans. David Hurst. Cistercian Studies Series 82. Kalamazoo, MI: Cistercian Publications, 1985.

Bengel, J. A. *Gnomon of the New Testament,* vol. 5. Trans. Andrew Fausset.

Edinburgh: T. & T. Clark, 1860.

Bennett, W. H. *The General Epistles: James, Peter, John, and Jude.* The Century Bible. Edinburgh: T.C. & E.C. Jack, 1901.

Benson, George. *A Paraphrase of the Seven (Commonly Called) Catholic Epistles.* London: J. Waugh, 1749.

Best, Ernest. *1 Peter.* New Century Bible. London: Oliphants, 1971.

Biggs, Charles. *A Critical and Exegetical Commentary on the Epistles of St. Peter and St. Jude.* The International Critical Commentary. 2nd ed. Edinburgh: T. & T. Clark, 1902.

Blenkin, G. W. *The First Epistle General of Peter.* Cambridge Greek Testament for Schools and Colleges. Cambridge: The University Press, 1914.

Boismard, M. E. *Quatre hymnes baptismale dans la première Épître de Pierre.* LD 30. Paris: Cerf, 1961.

Bokser, Ben Zion. *Pharisaic Judaism in Transition: R. Eliezer the Great and Jewish Reconstruction After the War with Rome.* New York, NY: Bloch Publishing Company, 1935 [reprinted in "The Jewish People: History, Religion, Literature" series by Arno Press Inc., 1973].

Briscoe, Stuart. *1 Peter: Holy Living in a Hostile World.* Rev. ed. Wheaton, IL: Shaw Publications, 1993 [1982].

Brown, John. *Expository Discourses on the First Epistle of the Apostle Peter.* 3 vols. New York, NY: Robert Carter & Brothers, 1851 [reprinted; Evansville, IN: The Sovereign Book Club, 1956].

Brox, Norbert. *Der erste Petrusbrief.* Evangelisch-katholischer Kommentar zum Neuen Testament 21. Zürich: Benziger Verlag, 1979.

Calloud, Jean and François Genuyt. *La première épître de Pierre: Analyse semiotique.* LD 109. Paris: Cerf, 1982.

Calvin, John. *Commentaries on the Catholic Epistles.* Trans. John Owen. Grand Rapids, MI: Eerdmans, 1948 [Edinburgh: T. Constable, 1855].

Campbell, Douglas A. *The Rhetoric of Righteousness in Romans 3.21-26.* JSNTSuppl. 65. Sheffield: JSOT Press, 1992.

Causse, A. *Les dispersés d'Israël: Les origines de la diaspora et son rôle dans la formation du judaïsme*. Études D'Histoire et de Philosophie Religieuses Publiées par la Faculté de Théologie Protestante de l'Université de Strasbourg 19. Paris: Librarire Félix Alcan, 1929.

Champion, L. G. *Benedictions and Doxologies in the Epistles of Paul*. Oxford: Kemp Hall Press, 1934.

Chester, Andrew and Ralph P. Martin. *The Theology of the Letters of James, Peter, and Jude*. New Testament Theology. Cambridge: Cambridge University Press, 1994.

Clark, Gordon H. *New Heaven, New Earth: A Commentary on First and Second Peter*. 2nd ed. Jefferson, MD: The Trinity Foundation, 1993.

Couard, Hermann. *Die Briefe des Petrus, Judas und Johannes*. Postsdam: August Stein, 1895.

Craddock, Fred B. *First and Second Peter and Jude*. Westminster Bible Companion. Louisville, KY: Westminster/John Knox Press, 1995.

Cranfield, C. E. B. *The First Epistle of Peter*. London: SCM Press Ltd., 1950.

_____. *I & II Peter and Jude*. Torch Bible Commentaries. London: SCM Press Ltd., 1960.

Cross, F. L. *1 Peter: A Paschal Liturgy*. 2nd ed. London: A. R. Mowbray, 1957.

Dalton, William J. *Christ's Proclamation to the Spirits*. Analecta Biblica 23. Rome: Pontifical Biblical Institute, 1965.

Daniélou, Jean. *Sacramentum Futuri: Études sur les origines de la typologie biblique*. Paris: Beauchesne et ses Fils, 1950.

_____. *From Shadows to Reality: Studies in the Biblical Typology of the Fathers*. Trans. Dom Wulstan Hibberd. London: Burns & Oates, 1960.

Davids, Peter H. *The First Epistle of Peter*. New International Commentary on the New Testament. Grand Rapids, MI: Eerdmans, 1990.

Demarest, John T. *Commentary on the Catholic Epistles*. New York, NY: Board of Publication of the Reformed Church in America, 1879.

Denniston, J. D. *The Greek Particles*. 2nd ed. Oxford: The Clarendon Press, 1959.

Doty, William G. *Letters in Primitive Christianity*. Guides to Biblical Scholarship: New Testament Series. Philadelphia, PA: Fortress Press, 1973.

Dunn, James D. G. *Christology in the Making: A New Testament Inquiry into the Origins of the Doctrine of the Incarnation*. Philadelphia, PA: Westminster Press, 1980.

Elliott, John H. *The Elect and the Holy*. Supplements to Novum Testamentum 12. Leiden: E. J. Brill: 1966.

_____. *A Home for the Homeless: A Sociological Exegesis of 1 Peter, its Situation and Strategy*. Philadelphia, PA: Fortress, 1981.

Eerdman, Charles R. *The General Epistles: An Exposition*. Philadelphia, PA: Westminster Press, 1918.

Pseudo-Euthalius. "Elenchus Capitum septem Epistolarum Catholicarum," in *Patrologia Graeca*, ed. J. P. Migne, vol. 85, 679-82.

Exler, Francis Xavier J. *The Form of the Ancient Greek Letter: A Study of Greek Epistolography*. Washington, D.C.: Catholic University of America, 1923.

Foster, Ora Delmer. *The Literary Relations of the First Epistle of Peter*. Transactions of the Connecticut Academy of Arts and Sciences 17. New Haven, CT: Yale University Press, 1913.

Funk, Robert W. *Language, Hermeneutic, and Word of God*. New York, NY: Harper & Row, 1966.

Gärtner, B. *The Temple and the Community in Qumran and in the New Testament*. SNTSMS 1. Cambridge: Cambridge University Press, 1965.

Gerhard, Johann. *Commentarius super Priorem D. Petri Epistolam*. Hamburg: Zacharia Hertelius, 1709.

Glasgow, Samuel McPheeters. *The General Epistles: Studies in the Letters of James, Peter, John and Jude*. Brief Book Studies. New York, NY: Fleming H. Revell Company, 1928.

Gloag, Paton J. *Introduction to the Catholic Epistles*. Edinburgh: T. & T. Clark, 1887.

Goebel, Siegfried. *Die Briefe des Petrus, griechisch, mit kurzer Erklärung*. Gotha: Friedrich Andreas perthes, 1893.

Goppelt, Leonard. *Typos. The Typological Interpretation of the Old Testament in the New.* Trans. Donald H. Madvig. Grand Rapids, MI: Eerdmans, 1982.

_____. *A Commentary on 1 Peter.* Trans. John E. Alsup. Grand Rapids, MI: Eerdmans, 1993.

Grudem, Wayne. *The First Epistle of Peter.* Tyndale New Testament Commentaries. Grand Rapids, MI: Eerdmans, 1989.

Haran, Menahem. *Temples and Temple-Service in Ancient Israel: An Inquiry into the Character of Cult Phenomena and the Historical Setting of the Priestly School.* Oxford: Clarendon Press, 1978.

Harnack, A. von. *Die Chronologie der altchristlichen Literatur bis Eusebius.* Leipzig, 1897.

Harris, J. R. *Testimonies.* Cambridge: Cambridge University Press, 1916.

Hauck, Friedrich. *Die Briefe des Jakobus, Petrus, Judas und Johannes.* 8th ed. Das Neue Testament Deutsch 10. Göttingen: Vandenhoeck & Ruprecht, 1957.

Pseudo-Hilarius Arelatensis. "Exposito in epistolas catholicas," in *Patrologia Latina*, ed. J. P. Migne, Supplement 3, 83-106.

Hillyer, Norman. *1 and 2 Peter, Jude.* NIBC 16. Peabody, MA: Hendrickson, 1992

Holzmeister, Urbanus. *Commentarius in Epistulas SS. Petri et Judae Apostolorum,* Cursus Scripturae Sacrae. Paris: P. Lethielleux, 1937.

Horneius, Conrad. *In epistolam catholicam sancti apostoli Petri priorem expositio litteralis.* Braunschweig: Duncker, 1654.

Hort, F. J. A. *The First Epistle of St. Peter: I.1-II.17.* London: Macmillan and Co., Limited, 1898.

Hunt, A. S. and C. C. Edgar. Trans., *Select Papyri.* 5 vols. LCL. Cambridge, MA: Harvard University Press, 1977.

Hunter, A. M. and E. G. Homrighausen. *The Epistle of James, The First and Second Epistles of Peter, The First, Second, and Third Epistles of John, The Epistle of Jude, The Revelation of St. John the Divine.* IB 12, Nashville, TN: Abingdon, 1957.

Hurd, John C. *The Origin of 1 Corinthians*, 2nd ed. Macon, GA: Mercer University Press, 1983 [1965].

Huther, J. E. *Kritisch-exegetisches Handbuch über den 1. Brief des Petrus, den Brief des Judas und den 2. Brief des Petrus.* Kritisch-exegetischer Kommentar über das Neue Testament 12. Göttingen: Vandenhoeck und Ruprecht, 1851.

Jachmann, Karl Reinhold. *Commentar über die katholischen Briefe mit genauer Berücksichtigung der neuesten Auslegungen.* Leipzig: Johann Ambrosius Barth, 1838.

Johnston, Robert. *The First Epistle of Peter: Revised Text with Introduction and Commentary.* Edinburgh: T. & T. Clark, 1888 [reprinted: Minneapolis, MN: James Family Publishing Company, 1978].

Jülicher, A. *Einleitung in das Neue Testament.* 7th ed. Tübingen: J. C. B. Mohr (Paul Seibeck), 1931.

Kelly, J. N. D. *A Commentary of the Epistles of Peter and Jude.* Black's New Testament Commentaries. London: A. and C. Black, 1969.

Kelly, William. *The First Epistle of Peter.* London: T. Weston, 1904.

Kennedy, George A. *New Testament Interpretation through Rhetorical Criticism.* Chapel Hill/London: The University of North Carolina Press, 1984.

_____. *Greek Rhetoric Under Christian Emperors.* Princeton, NJ: Princeton University Press, 1983.

_____. *Classical Rhetoric and Its Christian and Secular Tradition from Ancient to Modern Times.* Chapel Hill, NC: The University of North Carolina Press, 1980.

_____. *The Art of Rhetoric in the Roman World.* Princeton, NJ: Princeton University Press, 1972.

_____. *The Art of Persuasion in Greece.* Princeton, NJ: Princeton University Press, 1963.

Ketter, Peter. *Hebräerbrief, Jakobusbrief, Petrusbriefe, Judasbrief.* Die Heilige Schrift für das Leben erklärt 16.1. Freiburg: Herder, 1950.

Kim, Chan-Hie. *The Familiar Letter of Recommendation*. SBLDS 4. Missoula, MT: University of Montana, 1972.

Kistemaker, Simon J. *Exposition of the Epistles of Peter and of the Epistle of Jude*. New Testament Commentary, Grand Rapids: Baker Book House, 1987.

Kögel, Julius. *Die Gedankeneinheit des Ersten Briefes Petri*. Beiträge zur Förderung christlicher Theologie 6. Gütersloh: C. Bertelsmann, 1902.

Koskenniemi, Hiekki. *Studien zur Idee und Phraseologie des grieschischen Briefes bis 400 n. Chr.* Soumalaisen Tiedeakatemain Toimituksia; Annales Academiae Scientiarum Fennicae 102.2. Helsinki: Akateminen Kirjakauppa, 1956.

Kühl, Ernst. *Die Briefe Petri und Judae*. Kristisch-exegetischer Kommentar über das Neue Testament 12. 5th ed., Göttingen: Vandenhoeck & Ruprecht, 1887.

Kümmel, Werner Georg. *Introduction to the New Testament*. Trans. A. J. Mattil, 14th rev. ed. Nashville/New York: Abingdon, 1966.

Leaney, A. R. C. *The Letters of Peter and Jude*. CBC. Cambridge: Cambridge University Press, 1967.

Leighton, Robert. *Commentary on First Peter*. Grand Rapids, MI: Kregel Publications, 1972.

Lenski, R. C. H. *The Interpretation of the Epistles of St. Peter, St. John and St. Jude*. Columbus, OH: The Wartburg Press, 1945.

Lilje, Hanns. *Die Petrusbriefe und der Judasbrief*. Bibelhilfe für die Gemeinde Neutestamentliche Reihe 14, Kassel: J. G. Oncken, 1938.

Luther, Martin. "Sermons on the First Epistle of St. Peter," trans. Martin H. Bertram, 3-145; in *Luther's Works*, vol. 30: *The Catholic Epistles*. Saint Louis, MO: Concordia Publishing House, 1967.

Mack, Burton. *Rhetoric and the New Testament*. Guides to Biblical Scholarship. Minneapolis, MN: Fortress Press, 1990.

Margot, Jean-Claude. *Les Épîtres de Pierre*. Genève: Édition Labor et Fides, 1960.

Marshall, I. Howard. *1 Peter*. The IVP New Testament Commentary Series. Downers Grove, IL: InterVarsity Press, 1991.

Martin, Troy W. *Metaphor and Composition in 1 Peter*. SBLDS 131. Atlanta, GA: Scholars Press, 1992.

Martinus Legionensis. "Expositio in epistolam I B. Petri apostoli," in *Patrologia Latina*, ed. J. P. Migne, vol. 209, 217-52.

Masterman, John Howard Bertram. *First Epistles of S. Peter*. London: Macmillan and Co., 1900.

Mayerhoff, E. T. *Historische-critische Einleitung in die petrinischen Schriften*. Hamburg: Friedrich Perthes, 1835.

McKelvey, R. J. *The New Temple: The Church in the New Testament*. Oxford Theology Monographs. Oxford: Oxford University Press, 1969.

Metzner, Rainer. *Die Rezeption des Matthäusevangeliums im 1. Petrusbrief.* WUNT 2.74. J.C.B. Mohr (Siebeck), 1995.

Michaels, J. Ramsey. *1 Peter*. WBC 49. Waco, TX: Word Books, 1988.

Michl, Johann. *De Katholischen Briefe*. Das Neue Testament 8.2. Regensburg: Priedrich Pustet, 1953.

Miller, Donald G. *On This Rock: A Commentary on First Peter*. PTMS. Allison Park, PA: Pickwick Publications, 1993.

Mitton, C. L. *The Epistle to the Ephesians*. Oxford: The Clarendon Press, 1951.

Moffatt, James. *The General Epistles: James, Peter, and Judas*. The Moffatt New Testament Commentary. London: Hodder and Stoughton, 1947.

Monnier, Jean. *La Première Épître de l'Apôtre Pierre*. Macon: Protat Frères, 1900.

Moorehead, William G. *Outline Studies in the New Testament*. Pittsburgh: United Presbyterian Board of Publication, 1910.

Morus, S. F. N. *Praelectiones in Jacobi et Petri epistolas*. Leipzig: Sumptibus Sommeri, 1794.

Moulton, James H. *A Grammar of New Testament Greek*. 3 Vols. Edinburgh: T.& T. Clark, 1963.

Munro, W. *Authority in Paul and Peter. The Identification of a Pastoral Stratum in the Pauline Corpus and 1 Peter*. SNTSMS 45. Cambridge: Cambridge University Press, 1983.

Pseudo-Oecumenius. *Commentarii in epistolas catholicas*. In *Patrologia Graeca*. Edited by J. P. Migne. Vol. 119, 509-578.

Origen. *Homilies on Leviticus 1-16*, in *The Fathers of the Church* 83. Trans. Gary Wayne Barkley. Washington, D.C.: The Catholic University of America Press, 1990.

Perdelwitz, R. *Die Mysterienreligion und das Problem des ersten Petrusbriefes*. Religionsgeschichtliche Versuche und Vorarbeiten XI.3. Giessen, 1911.

Perkins, Pheme. *First and Second Peter, James, and Jude*. Interpretation. Louisville, KY: Westminster/John Knox Press, 1995.

Plumptre, E. H. *The General Epistles of St. Peter & St. Jude*. The Cambridge Bible for Schools and Colleges. Cambridge: Cambridge University Press, 1899.

Pury, Roland De. *Pierres vivantes*. Paris: Delachaux & Nestlé, 1944.

Quintilian, Marcus Fabius. *The Institutio Oratoria of Quintilian*. Trans. H. E. Butler. 4 Vols. LCL. Cambridge, MA: Harvard University Press, 1953.

Rendtorff, Heinrich. *Getrostes Wandern: Eine Einführung in den ersten Brief des Petrus*. Die urchristliche Botschaft 20. Hamburg: Furche, 1951.

Reicke, Bo. *The Disobedient Spirits and Christian Baptism*. Acta Seminarii Neotestamentici Upsaliensis 13. Kopenhagen: Einar Munksgaard, 1946.

_____. *The Epistles of James, Peter, and Jude*. AB 37. Garden City, NY: Doubleday & Co., 1964.

Robertson, A. T. *A Grammar of the Greek New Testament in the Light of Historical Research*. Nashville, TN.: Broadman Press, 1934.

Robinson, James M., ed. *The Nag Hammadi Library in English*. 3rd ed., revised. San Francisco, CA: HarperCollins, 1988.

Rogers, John. *A Godly & Fruitful Exposition Upon all the First Epistle of Peter.* London: Printed by John Field, 1650.

Scharfe, E. *Die Petrinische Strömung der Neutestamentlichen Literatur.* Berlin, 1893.

Schelkle, K. H. *Die Petrusbriefe, Der Judasbrief.* Herders Theologischer Kommentar zum Neuen Testament, 13.2. Freiburg: Herder, 1961.

Schiwy, Günther. *Weg ins Neue Testament.* Kommentar und Material, vol. 4, Nachpaulinen. Würzburg: Echter-Verlag, 1970.

Schneider, Johannes. *Die Briefe des Jakobus, Petrus, Judas, und Johannes.* Das Neue Testament Deutsch 10. Göttingen: Vandenhoeck & Ruprecht, 1961.

Schubert, Paul. *Form and Function of the Pauline Thanksgiving.* Beihefte zur Zeitschrift für die neutestamentliche Wissenschaft 20. Berlin: Alfred Töpelmann, 1939.

Schutter, William L. *Hermeneutic and Composition in 1 Peter.* WUNT 2.30. Tübingen: J. C. B. Mohr (Paul Siebeck), 1989.

Schweizer, Eduard. *Der erste Petrusbrief.* Prophezei, Zürich: Zwingli, 1942.

Selwyn, E. G. *The First Epistle of St. Peter.* London: Macmillan & Co., 1946; reprint, Thornapple Commentaries. Grand Rapids, MI: Baker Book House, 1981.

Serarius, Nicolus. *Prolegomena Bibliaca et Commentaria in omnes Epistolas Canonicas.* Paris: Balthasar Lippius, 1612.

Smyth, Herbert W. *Greek Grammar.* Cambridge, MA: Harvard University Press, 1956.

Spicq, Ceslas. *Les Épitres de Saint Pierre.* SB. Paris: Libraire Lecoffre, 1966.

Staffelbach, Georg. *Die Briefe der Apostel Jakobus und Judas, Petrus und Johannes.* Luzern: Räter & Cie, 1941.

Stendahl, K. *The School of St. Matthew and its Use of the Old Testament.* Acta Seminarii Neotestamentici Upsaliensis 20. Uppsala: C.W.K. Gleerup, 1954.

Stibbs, Alan M. *The First Epistle General of Peter.* The Tyndale New Testament Commentaries. Grand Rapids, MI: Eerdmans, 1959.

Stirewalt, M. Luther, Jr. *Studies in Ancient Greek Epistolography*. SBL Resources for Biblical Study 27. Atlanta, GA.: Scholars Press, 1993.

Streeter, Burnett Hillman. *The Primitive Church*. New York, NY: The Macmillan Co., 1929.

Thurén, Lauri. *The Rhetorical Strategy of 1 Peter: With Special Regard to Ambiguous Expressions*. Åbo, Akademis förlag,1990.

_____. *Argument and Theology in 1 Peter: The Origins of Christian Paraenesis*. JSNT Suppl. 114. Sheffield: Sheffield Academic Press, 1995.

Tomlyns, Samuel. *The Preaching of Christ, and the Prison of God, As the Certain Portion of them that reject Christ's Word. Opened in Several Sermons On I Peter III, 19*. London: Tho. Parkburst 1694.

Usteri, Johann Martin. *Wissenschaftlicher und Praktischer Commentar über den ersten Petrusbrief*. Zürich: S. Hohr, 1887.

Vanhoye, Albert. *La structure littéraire de l'Épître aux Hébreux*. Studia Neotestamentica 1. Paris: Desclée de Brouwer, 1962.

Vincent, Thomas. *The True Christian Love of the Unseen Christ: Or A Discourse chiefly tending to excite and promote the decaying Love of Christ in the Hearts of Christians*. London: Astwood and Samuel Sprint, 1689.

Wand, J. W. C. *The General Epistles of St. Peter and St. Jude*. Westminster Commentaries. London: Methuen & Co. Ltd., 1934.

Weidner, Revere F. *Annotations on the General Epistles of James, Peter, John, and Jude and the Revelation of St. John*. New York, NY: Charles Scribners Sons, 1905.

Weima, Jeffrey A. D. *Neglected Endings: The Significance of the Pauline Letter Closings*. JSNT Suppl. 101. Sheffield: JSOT Press, 1994.

Weiss, Bernard. *A Commentary on the New Testament*. Vol. 4: *Thessalonians to Revelation*. Trans. George Schodde and Epiphanius Wilson. New York, NY: Funk & Wagnalls Co., 1906.

Wenschlkewitz, H. *Die Spiritualisierung der Kultusbegriffe Tempel, Priester und Opfer im Neuen Testament (Angelos 4)*. Leipzig, 1932.

Wette, W. M. L. de. *Die katholischen Briefe, griechisch, mit kurzem Commentar*. Halle: Eduard Anton, 1847.

White, John L. *The Form and Function of the Body of the Greek Letter: A Study in the Letter-Body in the Non-literary Papyri and in Paul the Apostle*. SBLDS 2. Missoula, MT: University of Montana, 1972.

_____. *Light from Ancient Letters*. Philadelphia, PA: Fortress, 1986.

Windisch, H. and H. Preisker. *Die Katholischen Briefe*. Handbuch zum Neuen Testament, 15. 3rd ed. Tübingen, Kohr, 1951.

Winter, John. *Life and Letters in the Papyri*. Ann Arbor, MI: University of Michigan Press, 1933.

Zerwick, M. *Biblical Greek*. 4th edition. Trans. J. Smith. Rome: Scripta Pontifici instituti biblici, 1963.

Ziemann, P. *De Epistularum Graecarum Formulis Sollemnibus Quaestiones Selectae*. Berlin: Haas, 1912.

ARTICLES, PAPERS AND THESES

Achtemeier, Paul J. "Newborn Babes and Living Stones: Literal and Figurative in 1 Peter." In *To Touch the Text: Biblical and Related Studies in Honor of Joseph A Fitzmyer, S. J.* Ed. by Maurya P. Horgan and Paul J. Kobelski, 207-236. New York, NY: Crossroads, 1989.

Agnew, Francis H. "1 Peter 1:2 -- An Alternative Translation." *CBQ* 45 (1983): 68-73.

Aland, K. "The Problem of Anonymity and Pseudonymity in Christian Literature of the First Two Centuries." *JTS* 12 (1961): 39-49.

Applegate, Judith. "The Co-Elect Woman of 1 Peter." *NTS* 38(1992): 587-604.

Balch, David. "Early Christian Criticism of Patriarchal Authority: 1 Peter 2:11-3:12." *USQR* 39 (1984): 161-73.

_____. "Hellenization/Acculturation in 1 Peter." In *Perspectives on First Peter*. Ed. by Charles H. Talbert, 79-101. NABPR Special Studies 9 Macon, GA: Mercer University Press, 1986.

Beare, Francis Wright. "The Teaching of First Peter." *ATR* 27 (1945): 284-96.

Bechtler, Steven Richard. Review of T. Martin's *Metaphor and Composition in 1 Peter*, in *PrincSB* 14 (1993): 81-83.

Berger, Klaus. "Hellenistische Gattungen im Neuen Testament." *ANRW* 25.2 (1984): 1033-1431.

Bernas, Casimir. Review of T. Martin's *Metaphor and Composition in 1 Peter*, in *RSR* 19 (1993): 265.

Best, Ernest. "1 Peter II 4-10 -- A Reconsideration." *NovT* 11 (1969): 270-93.

Bethge, Hans-Gebhard. "Der Text des ersten Petrusbriefes im Crosby-Schøyen-Codex (Ms. 193 Schøyen Collection)." *ZNW* 84 (1993): 255-267.

Boismard, M. E. "Pierre (Première Epître de)." *Dictionnaire de la Bible*, Supplément 7: *Pastorales-Pirot*, 1415-55. Paris: Letouzey & Ané, 1966.

Boring, M. E. "Interpreting 1 Peter as a Letter [not] Written to Us." *QR* 13 (1993): 89-111.

Bornemann, W. "Der erste Petrusbrief: Eine Taufrede des Silvanus." *ZNW* 19 (1920): 143-65.

Botha, J. "Christian and Society in 1 Peter: Critical Solidarity." *Scriptura* 24 (1988): 27-37.

Bradley, David G. "The Origins of the Hortatory Material in the Letters of Paul." Ph.D. dissertation, Yale University, 1947.

Braun, Herbert. "Ποιέω," *Theological Dictionary of the New Testament.* Ed. by G. Kittel. Vol. 6:458-84. Grand Rapids, MI: Eerdmans, 1968.

Brooks, Oscar S. "1 Peter 3:21 -- The Clue to the Literary Structure of the Epistle." *NovT* 16 (1974): 290-305.

Brown, John Pairman. "Synoptic Parallels in the Epistles and Form-History." *NTS* 10 (1963-64): 27-48.

Bultmann, Rudolf. "Bekenntnis- und Liedfragmente im ersten Petrusbrief." *ConNT* 11 (1947): 1-14.

Callahan, Allen Dwight. "Paul's Epistle to Philemon: Toward an Alternative *Argumentum.*" *HTR* 86 (1993): 357-76.

Calloud, Jean. "Ce que parler veut dire (1 P 1, 10-12)." In *Étude sur la Première Lettre de Pierre.* LD 102. Ed. by Charles Perrot, 175-206. Paris: Cerf, 1980.

Cheung, Alex T. M. "The Priest As the Redeemed Man: A Biblical-Theological Study of the Priesthood." *JETS* 29 (1986): 265-75.

Chevallier, Alain. "I Pierre 1/1 à 2/10: Structure littéraire et conséquences exégétiques." *RHPR* 51 (1971): 129-42.

Chin, M. "A Heavenly Home for the Homeless. Aliens and Strangers in 1 Peter." *TynBul* 42 (1991): 96-112.

Combrink, H. J. B. "The Structure of 1 Peter." *Neot.* 9 (1975): 34-63.

Cook, David. "The Prescript as Programme in Galatians." *JTS* 43 (1992): 511-19.

Coutts, J. "Ephesians 1.3-14 and 1 Peter 1.3-12." *NTS* 8 (1956-57): 115-27.

Dalton, William J. "1 Peter 3:19 Reconsidered." In *The New Testament Age: Essays in Honor of Bo Reicke*, vol. 1. Ed. by William C. Weinrich, 95-105. Macon, GA: Mercer University Press, 1984.

_____. "Interpretation and Tradition: An Example from 1 Peter." *Greg* 49 (1968): 11-37.

Danker, Frederick W. "1 Peter 1.24-2.17 -- A Consolatory Pericope." *ZNW* 58 (1967): 93-103.

Davies, Charles T. "A Multidimensional Criticism of the Gospels." In *Orientation and Disorientation: Studies Presented in Honor of William A. Beardslee.* Ed. Richard J. Spencer, 87-98. PTMS 35. Pittsburgh: The Pickwick Press, 1980.

Davies, Paul E. "Primitive Christology in 1 Peter." In *Festschrift to Honor F. Wilbur Gingrich.* Ed. Howard Barth and Ronald Edwin Cocroft 115-22. Leiden: E. J. Brill, 1972.

Davids, Peter H. Review of T. Martin, *Metaphor and Composition in 1 Peter*, in *CBQ* 55 (1993): 594-95.

DeSilva, David A. "Despising Shame: A Cultural-Anthropological Investigation of the Epistle to the Hebrews." *JBL* 113 (1994): 438-61.

Desjardins, Michel. "The Portrayal of the Dissidents in 2 Peter and Jude: Does it Tell Us More About the 'Godly' than the 'Ungodly'?" *JSNT* 30 (1987): 89-102.

Detweiler, Robert. "After the New Criticism: Contemporary Methods of Literary Interpretation." In *Orientation and Disorientation: Studies Presented in Honor of William A. Beardslee*. Ed. by Richard J. Spencer, 3-23. PTMS 35. Pittsburgh: The Pickwick Press, 1980.

Dijkman, J. H. L. "The Socio-Religious Condition of the Recipients of I Peter: An Attempt to Solve the Problems of Date, Authorship and Addressees of the Letter." Ph.D. dissertation, University of Witwatersrand (Johannesburg, South Africa), 1984.

_____. "῞Οτι as an Introductory Formula to Catechetical References in 1 Peter." In *A South African Perspective on the New Testament: Essays by South African New Testament Scholars presented to Bruce Manning Metzger during his Visit to South Africa in 1985*. Ed. by J. H. Petzer and P.J. Hartin, 260-270. Leiden: E. J. Brill, 1986.

_____. "1 Peter: A Later Pastoral Stratum?" *NTS* 33 (1987): 265-271.

Downing, F. Gerald. "Pliny's Prosecutions of Christians: Revelation and 1 Peter." *JSNT* 34 (1988): 105-123.

Dungan, David L., "The Purpose and Provenance of the Gospel of Mark According to the 'Two Gospel' (Griesbach) Hypothesis." In *Colloquy on New Testament Studies: A Time for Reappraisal and Fresh Approaches*. Ed. by Bruce Corley, 131-56 ["Seminar Dialogue with David Dungan," pp. 157-79]. Macon, GA: Mercer University Press, 1983.

Elliott, John H. "Backward and Forward 'In His Steps': Following Jesus from Rome to Raymond and Beyond. The Tradition, Redaction, and Reception of 1 Peter 2:18-25." In *Discipleship in the New Testament*. Ed. by Fernando F. Segovia, 184-209. Philadelphia, PA: Fortress, 1985.

_____. "The Roman Provenance of 1 Peter and the Gospel of Mark: A Response to David Dungan." In *Colloquy on New Testament Studies: A Time for Reappraisal and Fresh Approaches*. Ed. by Bruce Corley, 181-94. Macon, GA: Mercer University Press, 1983.

_____. "The Rehabilitation of an Exegetical Step-Child: 1 Peter in Recent Research." *JBL* 95 (1976): 243-254.

_____. "1 Peter, Its Situation and Strategy: A Discussion with David Balch." In *Perspectives on First Peter*. Ed. by Charles H. Talbert, 61-78. NABPR Special Studies 9. Macon, GA: Mercer University Press, 1986.

_____. Review of R. Feldmeier, *Die Christen als Fremde: Die Metapher der Fremde in der antiken Welt, im Urchristentum im 1. Petrusbrief,* in *CBQ* 56 (1994): 79-793.

_____. "Disgraced Yet Graced. The Gospel according to 1 Peter in the Key of Honor and Shame." *BTB* 25 (1995): 166-78.

Ellul, D. "Un exemple de cheminement rhétorique: 1 Pierre." *RHPR* 70 (1990): 17-34.

Erickson, Millard J. "Is There Opportunity for Salvation After Death?" *BSac* 152 (1995): 131-144.

Evang, Martin. " Ἐκ καρδίας ἀλλήλους ἀγαπήσατε ἐκτενῶς: Zum Verständnis der Aufforderung und ihrer Begründungen in 1 Petr 1,22f." *ZNW* 80 (1989): 110-123.

Feinburg, John S. "1 Peter 3:18-20, Ancient Mythology, and the Intermediate State." *WTJ* 48 (1986): 303-336.

Ferguson, Everett. "Spiritual Sacrifices in Early Christianity and its Environment." *ANRW* 23.2 (1980): 1151-89.

Filson, Floyd V. "Partakers With Christ: Suffering in First Peter." *Int* 9 (1955): 400-12.

Fink, Paul R. "The Use and Significance of *en hō* in 1 Peter." *GJ* 8 (1967): 33-39.

Fiorenza, Elisabeth Schüssler. "Cultic Language in Qumran and in the NT." *CBQ* 38 (1976): 159-77.

Fitzmyer, Joseph A. "Some Notes on Aramaic Epistolography." *JBL* 93 (1974): 201-225.

Francis, Fred O. "The Form and Function of the Opening and Closing Paragraphs of James and 1 John." *ZNW* 61 (1970): 110-26.

Francis, J. "'Like Newborn Babes' -- The Image of the Child in 1 Peter 2:2-3" In
    *Studia Biblica 1978: III. Papers on Paul and Other New Testament
    Authors. Sixth International Congress on Biblical Studies, Oxford 3-7
    April 1978.* Ed. by E. A. Livingstone, 111-17. JSNTSup. 3.
    Sheffield: JSOT Press, 1980.

Funk, Robert W. "The Apostolic *Parousia*: Form and Significance." In *Church
    History and Interpretation: Studies Presented to John Knox*, 249-68. Ed.
    by Wm. R. Farmer, C. F. D. Moule, and R. R. Niebuhr. Cambridge:
    Cambridge University Press, 1967.

Glenny, W. Edward. "The Hermeneutics of the Use of the Old Testament in
    1 Peter." Ph.D. dissertation, Dallas Theological Seminary, 1987.

Green, G. L. "The Use of the Old Testament for Christian Ethics in 1 Peter."
    TynBul 41 (1990): 276-89.

Gross, Carl D. "Are the Wives of 1 Peter 3.7 Christians?" *JSNT* 57 (1989): 89-96.

Gundry, Robert H. "'Verba Christi' in 1 Peter: Their Implications Concerning the
    Authorship of 1 Peter and the Authenticity of the Gospel Tradition." *NTS*
    13 (1967): 336-50.

_____. "Further *Verba* on *Verba Christi* in First Peter." *Bib* 55 (1974): 211-32.

Hall, Robert G. "Isaiah's Ascent to See the Beloved: An Ancient Jewish Source
    for the *Ascension of Isaiah*?" *JBL* 113 (1994): 463-84.

Haran, Menahem. "Temple and Community in Ancient Israel." In *Temple in
    Society.* Ed. by Michael V. Fox, 17-25. Winona Lake, MN: Eisenbrauns,
    1988.

Harmon, G. M. "Peter: the Man and the Epistle." *JBL* 17 (1898): 31-39.

Hiebert, D. Edmond. "Designation of the Readers in 1 Peter 1:1-2." *BSac* 137
    (1980): 64-75.

Hill, David. "On Suffering and Baptism in 1 Peter." *NovT* 18 (1976): 181-89.

_____. "'To Offer Spiritual Sacrifices . . .' (1 Peter 2:5): Liturgical
    Formulations and Christian Paraenesis in 1 Peter." *JSNT* 16 (1982): 45-63.

Hobbie, Peter H. "1 Peter 2:2-10." *Int* 47 (1993): 170-73.

Jewett, Robert. "The Form and Function of the Homiletic Benediction." *ATR* 51 (1969) 18-34.

Johnson, Dennis E. "Fire in God's House: Imagery from Malachi 3 in Peter's Theology of Suffering (1 Pet 4:12-19)." *JETS* 29 (1986): 285-94.

Jonsen, Albert R. "The Moral Theology of the First Epistle of St. Peter." *ScEccl* 16 (1964): 93-105.

Katz, Albert N., *et al.* "Norms for 204 Literary and 260 Nonliterary Metaphors on 10 Psychological Dimensions." *Metaphor and Symbolic Activity* 3 (1988): 191-214.

Kayalaparampil, T. "Christian People, A Royal Priesthood (A Study on 1 Peter 2:9)." *Biblebhashyam* 15 (1989): 154-69.

Kendall, David W. "The Introductory Character of 1 Peter 1:3-12." Ph.D. dissertation, Union Theological Seminary, 1984.

_____. "The Literary and Theological Function of 1 Peter 1:3-12." In *Perspectives on First Peter*. Ed. by Charles H. Talbert, 103-20. NABPR Special Studies 9. Macon, GA: Mercer University Press, 1986.

Kennard, Douglas W. "Petrine Redemption: Its Meaning and Extent." *JETS* 30 (1987): 399-405.

Keyes, Clinton W. "The Greek Letter of Introduction." *AJP* 56 (1935): 28-44.

Klassen, William. "The Sacred Kiss in the New Testament: An Example of Social Boundary Lines." *NTS* 29 (1993): 122-35.

LaVerdiere, Eugene A. "A Grammatical Ambiguity in 1 Pet 1:23." *CBQ* 36 (1974): 89-94.

Légasse, S. "La soumission aux autorités d'après I Pierre 2.13-17: Version spécifique d'une parénèse traditionelle." *NTS* 34 (1988): 378-96.

Lehmann, Manfred. "The Key to Understanding the Copper Scroll: Where the Temple Tax Was Buried." *BAR* 19 (1993): 38-43.

_____. "Identification of the Copper Scroll Based on Its Technical Terms." *RevQ* 17 (1964): 97-105.

Lepelley, Claude. "Le contexte historique de la Première Lettre de Pierre: Essai d'interprétation." In *Étude sur la Première Lettre de Pierre*. Ed. by Charles Perrot, 43-64. LD 102. Paris: Cerf, 1980.

Lifkowitz, Mary R. "Metaphor and Simile in Ennius." *CJ* 55 (1959): 123-125.

Lips, Hermann von. "Die Haustafel als 'Topos' im Rahmen der urchristlichen Paränese: Beobachtungen anhand des 1. Petrusbriefes und des Titusbriefes." *NTS* 40 (1994): 261-80.

Lohse, Eduard. "Paränese und Kerygma im I. Petrusbrief." *ZNW* 45 (1954): 68-89.

_____. "Paranesis and Kerygma in 1 Peter." Translated by John Steely. In *Perspectives on First Peter*. Ed. by Charles H. Talbert, 37-59. NABPR Special Studies Series 9. Macon, GA.: Mercer University Press, 1986.

Love, Julian Prince. "The First Epistle of Peter." *Int* 8 (1954): 63-87.

Lumby, J. R. "I Peter III. 17." *Expositor* 5 (1890): 142-47.

Malherbe, Abraham J. "Exhortation in First Thessalonians." *NovT* 25 (1983): 238-56.

_____. "Ancient Epistolary Theory." *Ohio Journal of Religious Studies* 5 (1977): 63-71.

Martin, Ralph P. "The Composition of 1 Peter in Recent Study." In *Vox Evangelica: Biblical and Historical Essays*, 29-42. London: Epworth Press, 1962.

Martin, R. P. McGuire. "Letters and Letter Carriers in Christian Antiquity." *CW* 58 (1960): 148-200.

Martin, Troy W. "The Present Indicative in Petrine Prophetic Statements." Unpublished Paper presented at the Midwest Region of the Society of Biblical Literature, February 19, 1990.

_____. "The Present Indicative in the Eschatological Statements of 1 Peter 1:6, 8." *JBL* 111 (1992): 307-14.

_____. "Apostasy to Paganism: The Rhetorical Stasis of the Galatian Controversy." *JBL* 114 (1995): 437-61.

McCartney, Dan G. "λογικός in 1 Peter 2,2." *ZNW* 82 (1991): 237-50.

McCaughey, J. D. "Three 'Persecution Documents' of the New Testament."
     AusBR 17 (1969): 27-40.

McKay, K. L. "Aspect in Imperatival Constructions in New Testament Greek."
     NovT 27 (1985): 201-26.

McKelvey, R. J. "Christ the Cornerstone." *NTS* 8 (1961): 352-59.

McKnight, Edgar V. "The Contours and Methods of Literary Criticism." In
     *Orientation and Disorientation: Studies Presented in Honor of William A.
     Beardslee.* Ed. by Richard J. Spencer, 53-69. PTMS 35. Pittsburgh, PA:
     The Pickwick Press, 1980.

McNicol, Allan J. "The Eschatological Temple in the Qumran Pesher
     4QFlorilegium 1:1-7." *Ohio Journal of Religious Studies* 5 (1977): 133-41.

Michaels, J. Ramsey. "Eschatology in 1 Peter III. 17." *NTS* 13 (1966-67): 394-401.

_____. "Jewish and Christian Apocalyptic Letters: 1 Peter, Revelation, and 2
     Baruch 78-87." Ed. by Kent Harold Richards, 268-75. SBLSP 26 Atlanta,
     GA: Scholars Press, 1987.

_____. Review of Troy Martin's *Metaphor and Composition in 1 Peter*, in *JBL*
     112 (1993): 358-360.

Miller, Donald G. "Deliverance and Destiny: Salvation in First Peter." *Int* 9
     (1955): 413-25.

Moule, C. F. D. "Some Reflections on the 'Stone' *Testimonia* in Relation to the
     Name Peter." *NTS* 2 (1955): 56-58.

_____. "The Nature and Purpose of 1 Peter." *NTS* 3 (1956): 1-11.

Mullins, Terence V. "Disclosure: A Literary Form in the New Testament." *NovT*
     7 (1964): 44-50.

Murphy, Larry E. "The Concept of the Twelve in Luke-Acts as a Key to the
     Lukan Perspective on the Restoration of Israel." Ph.D. dissertation,
     Southern Baptist Theological Seminary, 1988.

Nixon, R.E. "The Meaning of 'Baptism' in 1 Peter 3,21." *Texte und
     Untersuchungen zur altchristlichen Literatur* 102 (1968): 437-41.

Osborne, T. P. "Guide Lines for Christian Suffering: A Source-Critical and Theological Study of 1 Peter 2:21-25." *Bib* 64 (1983): 381-408.

Oss, Douglas A. "The Interpretation of the 'Stone' Passages by Peter and Paul: A Comparative Study." *JETS* 32 (1989): 181-200.

Palmer, Clark Lyndon. "The Use of Traditional Materials in Hebrews, James, and 1 Peter." Ph.D dissertation, Southwestern Baptist Theological Seminary, 1985.

Parker, David C. "The Eschatology of 1 Peter." *BTB* 24 (1994): 27-32.

Pearson, Sharon Clark. "The Christological Hymnic Pattern in 1 Peter." Ph.D dissertation, Fuller Theological Seminary, 1993.

Perdue, Leo G. "Paraenesis and the Epistle of James." *ZNW* 72 (1981): 273-79.

Petersen, Norman R. "Literary Criticism in Biblical Studies." In *Orientation and Disorientation: Studies Presented in Honor of William A. Beardslee*. Ed. by Richard J. Spencer, 25-50. PTMS 35. Pittsburgh, PA: The Pickwick Press, 1980.

Pitch, John J. "'Visiting Strangers' and 'Resident Aliens.'" *TBT* 29 (1991): 357-61.

Plumpe, J. C. "VIVUM SAXUM, VIVI LAPIDES: The Concept of 'Living Stone' in Classical and Christian Antiquity." *Traditio* 1 (1943): 1-14.

Prigent, Pierre. "1 Pierre 2,4-10." *RHPR* 72 (1992): 53-60.

Refoulé, F. "Soumission et liberté." *Vie Spirituelle* 690 (1990): 331-42.

Reinarch, Theodore. "Diaspora." In *The Jewish Encyclopedia*. Vol. 4: *Chazars-Dreyfus*, 559-73. New York, NY: KTAV Publishing House, 1906.

Rensburg, J. J. Janse van. "The Use of Intersentence Relational Particles and Asyndeton in First Peter." *Neot* 24 (1990): 283-300.

Richard, Earl. "The Functional Christology of First Peter." In *Perspectives on First Peter*. Ed. by Charles H. Talbert, 121-39. NABPR Special Studies 9. Macon, GA: Mercer University Press, 1986.

Riesenfeld, Ernst Harald. "Περί." *Theological Dictionary of the New Testament*. Ed. by G. Kittel. Vol. 6:53-56. Grand Rapids, MI: Eerdmans, 1968.

Robertson, Gregory R. "The Use of Old Testament Quotations and Allusions in the First Epistle of Peter." M.A. thesis, Anderson School of Theology, Anderson University, 1990.

Russell, Ronald. "Eschatology and Ethics in 1 Peter." *EvQ* 47 (1975): 78-84.

Sandevoir, Pierre. "Un royaume de prêtres?" In *Étude sur la Première Lettre de Pierre.* Ed. by Charles Perrot, 219-29. LD 102. Paris: Cerf, 1980.

Scharlemann, M. H. "'He Descended into Hell.' An Interpretation of 1 Peter 3:18-20." *ConcorJ* 15 (1989): 311-22.

Schertz, Mary H. "Nonretaliation and the Haustafeln in 1 Peter." In *The Love of Enemy and Nonretaliation in the New Testament.* Ed. by William M. Swartley, 258-86. Studies in Peace and Scripture. Louisville, KY: Westminster/John Knox, 1992.

Schlosser, Jacques. "Ancien Testament et Christologie dans la *Prima Petri.*" In *Étude sur la Première Lettre de Pierre.* Ed. by Charles Perrot, 65-96. LD 102. Paris: Cerf, 1980.

Schmidt, David Henry. "The Peter Writings: Their Redactors and their Relationships." Ph.D. dissertation, Northwestern University (Evanston, IL), June 1972.

Schutter, William L. "1 Peter 4.17, Ezekiel 9.6, and Apocalyptic Hermeneutics." Ed. Kent Harold Richards, 276-84. SBLSP 26. Atlanta, GA: Scholars Press, 1987.

_____. Review of Reinhard Feldmeier's *Die Christen als Fremde: Die Metapher der Fremde in der antiken Welt, im Urchristentum im 1. Petrusbrief,* in *JBL* 113 (1994): 743-45.

Schweizer, Eduard. "The Priesthood of All Believers: 1 Peter 2.1-10." In *Worship, Theology and Ministry in the Early Church: Essays in Honor of Ralph P. Martin.* Ed. by Michael J. Wilkins and Terence Paige, 285-93. JSNT Supplement Series 87.Sheffield: JSOT Press, 1992.

Seland, Torrey. "The 'Common Priesthood' of Philo and 1 Peter: A Philonic Reading of 1 Peter 2.5,9." *JSNT* 57 (1995): 87-119.

Selwyn, E. G. "Eschatology in 1 Peter." In *The Background of the New Testament and its Eschatology: In Honour of Charles Harold Dodd.* Ed. by W. D. Davies and D. Daube, 394-401. Cambridge: Cambridge University

Press, 1964.

Shimada, Kazuhito. "The Formulary Material in First Peter: A Study According to the Method of *Traditionsgeschichte*." Th.D. dissertation, Union Theological Seminary, 1966.

_____. "Is 1 Peter Dependent on Ephesians? A Critique of C. L. Mitton." *AJBI* 17 (1991): 77-106.

_____. "Is 1 Peter Dependent on Romans?" *AJBI* 19 (1993): 87-137.

Slaughter, James R. "The Dynamics of Marriage in 1 Peter 3:1-7." Th.D. dissertation, Dallas Theological Seminary, 1992.

_____. "The Importance of Literary Argument for Understanding 1 Peter." *BSac* 152 (1995): 72-91.

_____. "Submission of Wives (1 Pet. 3:1a) in the Context of 1 Peter." *BSac* 153 (1996): 63-74 [part 1 of a 3 part series].

_____. "Winning Unbelieving Husbands to Christ (1 Pet. 3:1b-4)." *BSac* 153 (1996): 199-211 [part 2 of a 3 part series].

_____. "Sarah as a Model for Christian Wives (1 Pet. 3:5-6)." *BSac* 153 (1996): 357-65 [part 3 of a 3 part series].

Sly, Dorothy. "1 Peter 3:6b in the Light of Philo and Josephus." *JBL* 110 (1991): 126-29.

Snyder, Scot. "1 Peter 2:17: A Reconsideration." *FilologiaNT* 4 (1991): 211-15.

Talbert, Charles H. "Once Again: The Plan of 1 Peter." In *Perspectives on First Peter*. Ed. by Charles H. Talbert, 141-51. NABPR Special Studies 9. Macon, GA: Mercer University Press, 1986.

Thompson, James W. "The Rhetoric of 1 Peter." *ResQ* 36 (1994): 237-50.

Tite, Philip L. "Pax, Peace, and the New Testament." *Rel* 11 (1995): 301-24.

_____. "The Compositional Function of the Petrine Prescript: A Look at 1 Peter 1:1-3." *JETS* 39 (1996): 47-56.

Toit, A. B. du. "The Significance of Discourse Analysis for New Testament Interpretation and Translation: Introductory Remarks with Special

Reference to 1 Peter 1:2-13." *Neot* 8 (1974): 54-79.

Unnik, W. C. van. "The Teaching of Good Works in 1 Peter." *NTS* 1 (1954): 92-110.

_____. "A Classical Parallel to 1 Peter ii. 14 and 20." *NTS* 2 (1955): 198-202.

_____. "Christianity According to 1 Peter." *ExpTim* 68 (1956-1957): 79-83.

_____. "Peter, First Letter of." In *The Interpreters Dictionary of the Bible*, vol. 3: *K-Q*, 758-66, New York, NY: Abingdon Press, 1962.

_____. "The Critique of Paganism in 1 Peter 1:18." *Neotestamentica et Semitica's Studies in Honour of Matthew Black*. Ed. by E. Earle Ellis and Max Wilcox, 129-42. Edinburgh: T. & T. Clark, 1969.

VanHoye, Albert. "1 Pierre au carrefour des théologies du Nouveau Testament." In *Étude sur la Première Lettre de Pierre*. Ed. by Charles Perrot, 97-128. LD 102. Paris: Cerf, 1980.

Villiers, J. L. de. "Joy in Suffering in 1 Peter." *Neot* 9 (1975): 64-86.

Vos, Johan S. "Paul's Argumentation in Galatians 1-2." *HTR* 87 (1994): 1-16.

Wand, J. W. C. "The Lessons of First Peter: A Survey of Recent Interpretation." *Int* 9 (1955): 387-99.

Warden, Duane. "Imperial Persecution and the Dating of 1 Peter and Revelation." *JETS* 34 (1991): 203-12.

Webb, Robert L. "The Apocalyptic Perspective of First Peter." Th.M. thesis, Regent College, Vancouver, B.C., 1986.

White, John L. "The Structural Analysis of Philemon: A Point of Departure in the Formal Analysis of the Pauline Letter." Paper for the Society of Biblical Literature Seminar on the Form and Function of the Pauline Letters, 1971.

_____ (with Keith A. Kensinger). "Catagories of Greek Papyrus Letters," Ed. by George MacRae, 79-91. SBLSP 10. Missoula, MO: Scholars Press, 1976.

Wifstrand, Albert. "Stylistic Problems in the Epistles of James and Peter." *ST* 1 (1948): 170-82.

Winters, Bruce W. "The Public Honouring of Christian Benefactors: Romans 13.3-4 and 1 Peter 2.14-15." *JSNT* 34 (1988): 87-103.

_____. "'Seek the Welfare of the City': Social Ethics according to 1 Peter." *Themelios* 13 (1988): 91-94.

Young, Frances Y. "Temple, Cult, and Law in Early Christianity: A Study in the Relationship Between Jews and Christians in the Early Centuries." *NTS* 19 (1972/73): 325-38.

INDICES

INDEX NOMINUM

INDEX LOCORUM

CLASSICAL SOURCES

Rhetorica Ad Herenuim
3.16.28-24.40 ... 28
4.26.35 ... 75

Plato
    Apology
    23A ... 57
    41D ... 100

Quintilian
    Inst. Orat.
    3.5.5 ... 97
    3.5.6 ... 97
    3.5.7 ... 97
    3.5.7-9 ... 98
    3.5.8 ... 98, 101
    3.5.9-10 ... 98
    3.5-3.6 ... 97
    3.5.17-3.6.104 ... 98
    3.6.72 ... 98
    3.6,76 ... 98
    3.7 ... 98
    4.1.5 ... 52

Aristotle
    Rhetorica
    1.3.3-7 ... 54
    3.14 ... 53

Cicero
    De Officiis
    2.9-11 ... 108

JEWISH SOURCES

Exodus
12:11 ... 64, 65

Numbers
6:25-26 ... 44

Leviticus ... 89

2 Samuel
7:10 ... 66

Psalms
33:13-17 ... 95
34:13-17 ... 95

Jeremiah
29:4-23 ... 39

Isaiah
53-54 ... 104

Hosea
2 ... 27

Daniel
3:98 ... 48
4:1 ... 44
6:25 ... 44

Susanna
5 ... 111
42-43 ... 111
47 ... 111